Eyewitness Testimonies
Appeals From
The A-bomb Survivors

Third Edition

Hiroshima Peace Culture Foundation

On the cover

A drawing by Nori Kikuzaki, which won the Hiroshima Municipal Board of Education Prize in the 13th Children's Peace Drawings Competition, held in 1998 by this Foundation and the City of Hiroshima. Nori Kikuzaki was a second-year student at Hiroshima City Furuta Junior High School at the time.

Eyewitness Testimonies: Appeals from The A-bomb Survivors
Third Edition

Copyright © 1990, 2000, 2003 by the Hiroshima Peace Culture Foundation
All rights reserved.
First edition March 20, 1990
Second edition January 31, 2000
Third edition July 15, 2003
Edited & Published by the Hiroshima Peace Culture Foundation
1-2 Nakajima-chō Naka-ku, Hiroshima 730-0811, Japan
      Tel. (082) 241-5246
      Fax (082) 542-7941
      E-mail: hpcf @ pcf. city. hiroshima. jp

Printed by Nakamoto Sogo Printing Co., Ltd.

ISBN-4-938239-08-6 C0095

Foreword

Humankind and Nuclear Weapons Cannot Coexist Indefinitely

by President Tadatoshi Akiba
Hiroshima Peace Culture Foundation

On August 6, 1945, the 350,000 people of Hiroshima experienced the cruel tragedy of the world's first atomic bombing. The conditions inflicted by that bomb transcend the capacity of words and even pictures to convey. Only those who were here at the time can know the full reality, and the survivors of that horror know from their experience that nuclear weapons are incompatible with human life on Earth. Many have spent their lives appealing constantly, "Never again! Nuclear weapons must be banned and eliminated."

In this book, we present the thoughts, feelings, and memories of fifteen survivors (two of whom are now deceased). All have taken part in peace studies programs held by this Foundation, telling their A-bomb experiences to students who come to Hiroshima on school excursions.

In addition, because so many Koreans and other non-Japanese were exposed to the bomb, we present a chapter contributed by an expert in that field.

With the Cold War almost over, real steps have been taken toward disarmament, and nuclear arsenals have been reduced significantly. Yet, the US, Russia, and other nuclear powers maintain more than enough nuclear weapons to exterminate the human race. Furthermore, India and Pakistan have conducted nuclear tests, raising fears that the number of nuclear powers will increase. The world today needs to listen again to the A-bomb survivors and strengthen its collective resolve to abolish nuclear weapons.

This book presents only a few A-bomb experiences, but readers will encounter in its pages the survivors' fierce desire for peace. We hope it will inspire and assist you in your service to that noble cause.

I am profoundly grateful to all who contributed.

Contents

Chapter 3   Foreign Atomic Bomb Victims

Chapter 1

An Overview of the Atomic Bombing

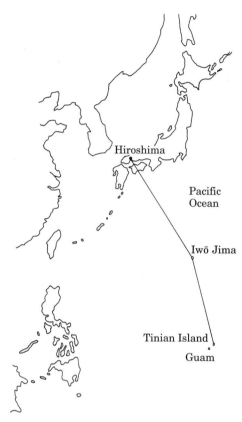

The Road that Led to the Atomic Bombing

Three B-29 bomber planes took off from Tinian Island to drop the atomic bomb on Hiroshima.

The B-29 "Enola Gay" dropped the atomic bomb.

The other two planes observed the explosion of the atomic bomb and took photographs.

Tinian is about 1,700 miles (2,740 kilometers) away from Hiroshima. The B-29 took 6 ½ hours each way.

Warning in Hiroshima prior to the dropping of the atomic bomb

Monday, August 6, 1945

    0:25 a.m. Air-raid warning* issued.

    2:10 a.m. Air-raid warning cleared.

    7:09 a.m. Yellow air-raid warning* issued.

    7:31 a.m. Yellow air-raid warning cleared.

    8:15 a.m. The atomic bomb was dropped just before the broadcasting of an air-raid warning was about to begin.

The Development and Production of the Atomic Bomb

Atoms are the basic components of materials. The central portion of an atom, the atomic nucleus, releases energy when it is artificially split. An atomic bomb uses such energy as a weapon.

The splitting of an atomic nucleus is called nuclear fission. As the figure shows, when one neutron collides with an atomic nucleus of uranium 235 or plutonium 239, several things happen. The nucleus breaks up into two parts which weigh almost the same, 2 or 3 neutrons are emitted, and energy is released. Next, these neutrons collide with other uranium 235 or plutonium 239 atomic nuclei and they also split in two, releasing neutrons and energy. When this nuclear fission occurs in a very rapid chain reaction, it produces very large amounts of energy.

Research on the atomic bomb started in Germany. However, the United States also immediately conducted research. Scientists started the project to produce the atomic bomb in 1942. This project was called by the secret code "Manhattan

Splitting of an atomic nucleus (nuclear fission)

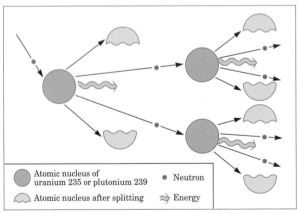

Atomic nucleus of uranium 235 or plutonium 239 ● Neutron

Atomic nucleus after splitting ⇒ Energy

Project," and was conducted at a huge cost. The United States succeeded in a test explosion of an atomic bomb in a desert near Alamogordo, New Mexico, for the first time in the history of mankind, on July 16, 1945.

On july 25, 1945, soon after the test succeeded, the following order to drop the atomic bomb was issued:

> The 509 Composite Group, 20th Air Force will deliver its first special bomb as soon as weather will permit visual bombing after about 3 August 1945 on one of the targets:
>
> Hiroshima, Kokura, Niigata, and Nagasaki.
>
> (abbreviated)

(Note) Later, Niigata was dropped from the list because, among other factors, it was too far away.

In accordance with this order, the atomic bomb was dropped on Hiroshima on August 6th. After that another bomb was dropped on Nagasaki on August 9th. Two cities were destroyed instantly and many lives were lost.

The Mechanism of the Atomic Bombs

(1) The Hiroshima Bomb

The Hiroshima Bomb used uranium 235. The bomb was divided into two parts. One part was designed to collide with the other part by the explosion of gunpowder, causing successive nuclear fission in quite a short time. This was called the "gun barrel method." The amount of energy released by this atomic bomb had never before been possible with gunpowder explosives.

The Hiroshima-type atomic bomb was long, cylindrical, and was called "Little Boy." Its energy was considered to be equiva-

The Hiroshima-type Bomb

Bomb design

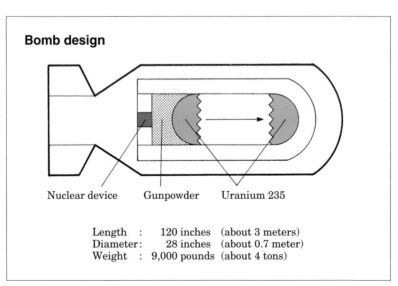

Nuclear device   Gunpowder   Uranium 235

Length   :   120 inches   (about 3 meters)
Diameter: 28 inches   (about 0.7 meter)
Weight   :   9,000 pounds   (about 4 tons)

lent to about 20 kilotons of TNT, but most recent research has estimated the yield to be the equivalent of about 16 kilotons.

The enormous energy released by nuclear fission was produced with only one kilogram of uranium 235 compacted in the bomb.

(2) The Nagasaki Bomb

The Nagasaki Bomb used plutonium 239. Nuclear fission occurred when plutonium 239 was pushed from its spherical casing toward the center by the pressure of surrounding gunpowder. This was called the "implosion method." Because the bomb was of a round type in comparison to the Hiroshima type, it was called "Fat Man."

The nuclear fission occurred in only one kilogram of plutonium 239. Its energy is considered to have been the equivalent of

The Nagasaki-type Bomb

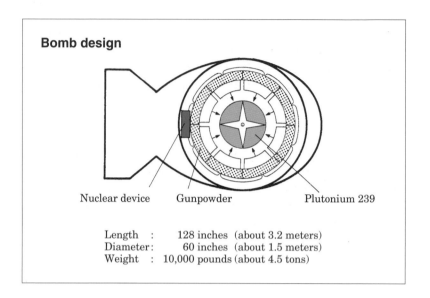

Bomb design

Nuclear device   Gunpowder   Plutonium 239

Length   :   128 inches (about 3.2 meters)
Diameter: 60 inches (about 1.5 meters)
Weight   :   10,000 pounds (about 4.5 tons)

about 21 kilotons of TNT.

History of Hiroshima

Hiroshima City developed on a delta area, which had been formed into land with earth and sand washed down by the Ōta River, filling in shallow areas of the sea over a long period of time.

About four hundred years ago Terumoto Mouri, the powerful feudal lord of the surrounding region built a castle on one of the delta islands and named this area "Hiroshima." Since then it prospered as a castle town, as well as an economic and transportation center. Through the Edo era (1603 – 1867) people reclaimed and created new land, and the town basically took on its present appearance.

As the Meiji era (1868 – 1912) began, armed forces were placed in Hiroshima before other locations. Afterwards, many military

Hiroshima Castle (prewar)

installations related to armed forces were set up, and
Hiroshima became a military base which sent troop overseas,
particularly in the Sino-Japanese War (1894 – 1895) and the
Russo-Japanese War (1904 – 1905). The town of Hiroshima developed with a close connection to the army, so it was called a
military city. Moreover, as many schools were established, it
was also called an educational city.

Hiroshima before the Bomb

On the morning of August 6th, the skies were perfectly clear without a speck of cloud. As the midsummer sun rose, the temperature also began to rise rapidly. When a yellow air-raid warning, issued at 7:09 a.m., was cleared at 7:31 a.m., the citizens gave a sigh of relief and started their activities. Many people had entered the city from neighboring towns and villages for building demolition* work. About 350,000 people are believed to have been in the city on that day, including more than 40,000 military personnel.

There was no vacation for students during war time. Students in upper grades of national (elementary) and middle-level schools (junior high, girls' high (or secondary) schools, and vocational schools) and above were working day after day in factories and at building demolition sites. On that day, a total of about 8,400 students were working on building demolition. Elementary school children in the third to the sixth grades were urged to evacuate to the countryside for protection from the air-raids. Mainly younger children in the first and second grades had remained in the city with their families.

Release and Detonation

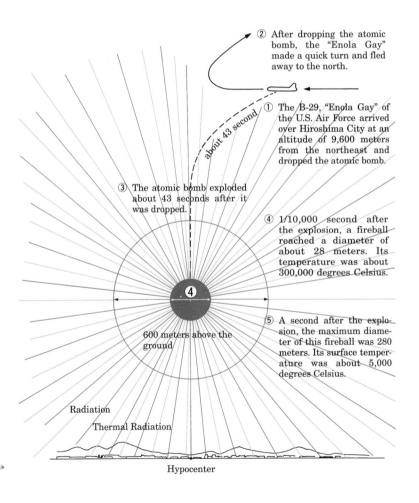

② After dropping the atomic bomb, the "Enola Gay" made a quick turn and fled away to the north.

① The B-29, "Enola Gay" of the U.S. Air Force arrived over Hiroshima City at an altitude of 9,600 meters from the northeast and dropped the atomic bomb.

about 43 second

③ The atomic bomb exploded about 43 seconds after it was dropped.

④ 1/10,000 second after the explosion, a fireball reached a diameter of about 28 meters. Its temperature was about 300,000 degrees Celsius.

④

600 meters above the ground

⑤ A second after the explosion, the maximum diameter of this fireball was 280 meters. Its surface temperature was about 5,000 degrees Celsius.

Radiation

Thermal Radiation

Hypocenter

Huge atomic cloud (photo from one of the three B29s which participated in the raid. Taken about one hour after the bombing from a point 80 kilometers from Hiroshima over the Seto Inland Sea.)　　(Photo by US Army)

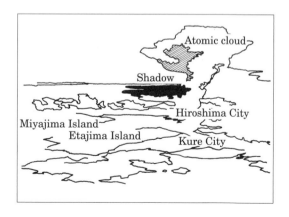

When the Bomb Exploded

Distribution of energy caused by the explosion

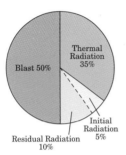

Blast 50%
Thermal Radiation 35%
Initial Radiation 5%
Residual Radiation 10%

The building now called "Atomic Bomb Dome" was formerly the Hiroshima Prefectural Industrial Promotion Hall. To the west of this building there is a unique T-shaped bridge (Aioi Bridge). This bridge is located in the center of Hiroshima City and even at present plays an important role as a bridge linking the east and west of the city with the southern area. This unique bridge is said to have been the target for the atomic bomb.

Research shows that the bomb exploded at an altitude of 600 meters above the

Former Hiroshima Prefectural Industrial Promotion Hall

Shima Hospital, about 300 meters southeast of this bridge. The hypocenter is the area directly below the spot where the bomb detonated in the air. Seen 9 kilometers from the detonation point, the fireball formed at the instant of the explosion was about 10 times brighter than the sun. From the fireball, intense heat rays and radiation were emitted in all directions. With the heat, the surrounding air greatly expanded and spread out as a blast. Thirty-five percent of the total energy which caused damage with the explosion was thermal radiation, 50% blast pressure, and 15% radiation.

Ruins of the Hiroshima Prefectural Industrial Promotion Hall (160 meters from the hypocenter).
Now called the A-bomb Dome, this building is a registered UNESCO World Heritage site, an international symbol of the horror of nuclear weapons and the necessity of peace. (Photo by US Army)

The expanse of rubble in Nakajima-honmachi (now Peace Memorial Park) seen from Ōte-machi.
The crushed building in the center was the Hiroshima Gas Company head office (210 meters from the hypocenter). The building to the right was the Bankers' Club. (Photo by US Army)

Damage from Heat Rays

The detonation point reached a temperature of several million degrees Celsius at the explosion of the atomic bomb. Surrounding air heated and formed a fireball. This ball reached a diameter of about 280 meters. The intense heat rays emitted in all directions from the fireball damaged everything in a very short time.

The temperature of the heat rays in the hypocenter is estimated to have been from 3,000 to 4,000 degrees Celsius. Within a radius one kilometer from the hypocenter, most of the people outdoors died not only with their skin totally burnt but also with their internal organs ruptured. Even about 3.5 kilometers away from the hypocenter, people suffered burns.

Thermal radiation effects were seen on various objects as well as on the human body. Within 600 meters from the hypocenter glass-like bubbles were formed on the surface of roof-tiles. Those parts of tiles sheltered by other tiles showed no change. The surface of granite stones exposed to heat rays within one kilometer of the hypocenter became sandy and whitish, and the quartz in the stones split open in pieces. Since clothes burn easily, the heat rays ignited them up to two kilometers away from the hypocenter.

Fires were caused by the intense heat rays and also by kitchen fires. Because the fires broke out simultaneously everywhere in the city, a conflagration occurred 30 minutes after the explosion. Everything combustible within a radius of two kilometers from the hypocenter burned completely.

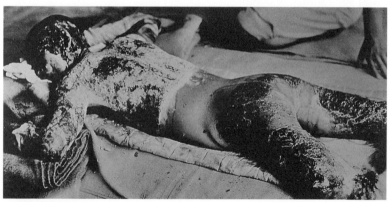

Totally burned
Except for a small area which was covered with a cloth wrapped about his waist, this man was burned all over his back.
(Less than 1 kilometer from the hypocenter)　　　(Photo by Masami Onuka)

Shadow of valve imprinted on a gas tank
Black coal tar on the surface of the tank made a clear shadow of the valve,
while the rest completely melted down.
(2 kilometers from the hypocenter)   (Photo by Shunkichi Kikuchi)

Damage from the Shock Wave and Blast

At the moment of the explosion, there was a huge expansion of
air caused by the heat. High pressure air (a shock wave) expanded in all directions like an invisible wall. The shock wave
caused great damage to everything on the ground, with the
wave coming directly from the explosion above, and then re-
bounding off from the ground and buildings. Directly following
this wall of pressure, an exceedingly strong blast of air rushed
through, causing further destruction. In the hypocenter the
force of the blast was equal to 440 meters per second. As the
blast spread outward, its force became weaker, but even at a
distance of about 2.3 kilometers from the hypocenter around the
Miyuki Bridge, its velocity was 45 meters per second. All the

stone railings of this bridge fell down.

People were blown several meters by the blast and a number of them were injured by broken glass fragments, some of which penetrated their skin. A great number of people were also burned to death, trapped in buildings blown down by the blast.

Damage done to the buildings was also great. Concrete buildings around the hypocenter were severely destroyed with the ceilings crashing down, windows and doors blown away. All wooden houses within a radius of about 2 kilometers from the

Destroyed building (Main Office of the Hiroshima Gas Corporation)
Buildings near the hypocenter made even of concrete were demolished by the strong pressure. (210 meters from the hypocenter)
(Photo by Shigeo Hayashi)

The destroyed main building of a temple
Even at a distance of 3.3 kilometers from the hypocenter, this temple was destroyed by the blast. (Photo by Shunkichi Kikuchi)

hypocenter were crushed, and even those far away were partially damaged.

Damage from Radiation

The atomic bomb is characterized by the extraordinarily great energy emitted at the explosion and the release of radiation which causes long-term damage to the human body. These characteristics are different from conventional bombs which use gunpowder as an explosive. The radiation released in large amounts within one minute of the explosion was called initial radiation. The radiation of the atomic bomb consisted of alpha rays, beta rays, gamma rays and neutrons, out of which mainly gamma rays and neutrons reached the ground. This radiation

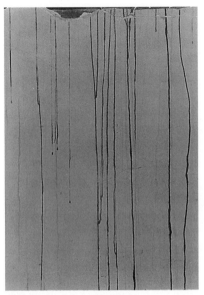

"Black rain" left behind on the white wall of a dwelling
(3.5 kilometers from the hypocenter)

had considerable effects on the human body. Most of those who were exposed to initial radiation within one kilometer of the hypocenter died.

Residual radiation (it is released from the soil and from roof-tiles which were made radioactive from the initial radiation) was present on the ground for a long period of time starting from one minute after the explosion. Those who were not directly exposed to the explosion but entered the area around the hypocenter on rescue and re-

lief activities or in search of relatives were affected by radiation.

After the explosion, the huge mushroom cloud rose up. For 20 or 30 minutes after the explosion, this cloud was blown by wind to the north-western part of the city, where "black rain"* fell. The black rain contained mud and dust blown up at the time of the explosion, soot from the resulting fires, and also radioactive substances.

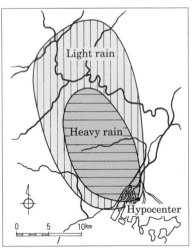

The range of "black rain" fall

24

Even in remote areas far from the hypocenter, the effects caused by radioactivity were seen.

Acute and Long-term Injury to the Human Body

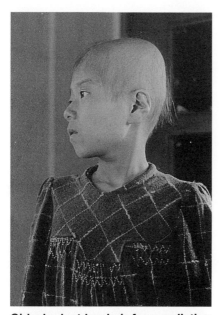

Girl who lost her hair from radiation (exposed in Funairi-chō, 1 kilometer from the hypocenter, began to lose hair two months after the bombing.)
(Photo by Shunkichi Kikuchi)

The three types of energy which caused widespread damage to property also caused tremendous injuries to people: burns from thermal radiation and fire, injuries from the blast, and sickness from radiation. The atomic bomb is characterized by the fact that even today, more than fifty years since the explosion, the effects of radiation continue.

All has not been revealed yet as to the effects of radiation on the human body, but we do know that people exposed to radiation suffer from various illnesses.

These can be categorized into acute sickness and long-term illness. Sickness which developed within 5 months from the time of the explosion was considered "acute." Symptoms of acute sickness were fever, nausea, diarrhea, bleeding from the nose and the mouth, epilation[1] and general malaise.[2]

Even after acute sickness had come to an end, the effects of the atomic bomb explosion continued. Long-term illness such as

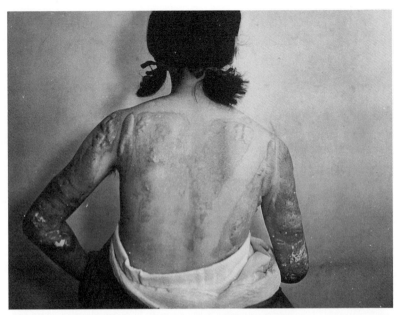

A Woman with Keloids on Her Back and Both Arms
This woman's bare arms were exposed and badly burned. Keloids developed over the scars. The only area left unburned was the diagonal stripe descending from her right shoulder where the strap of her handbag protected the skin. (Photo by US Army)

keloids[3] and leukemia[4] appeared. The incidence of leukemia peaked in the year from 1950 to 1953. Incidence of lung cancer and thyroid cancer increased from about 1960, after the incidence of leukemia had passed its peak.

As for the genetic effects of radiation, studies are being continued even at present but all details are not known.

[1] Epilation is the loss of hair by the roots.
[2] General malaise is a vague feeling of weakness or lack of health.
[3] Keloid is an overgrowth of scar tissue following a burn.
[4] Leukemia is a disease in which white blood cells greatly increase.

Number of Deaths due to the Atomic Bombing

The exact number of deaths due to the atomic bomb is still unknown today, partly because records of how many people were living in the city at that time, disappeared in the explosion and sufficient studies could not be conducted in the confusion after the bombing.

Deaths include more than those who died instantly in the explosion. During the first five months after the explosion many people died from exposure to the radiation. Even at present various studies are being conducted to investigate the total number of deaths. Some figures have been released regarding the number of deaths but so far about 140,000 (±10,000) people are considered to have died by the end of December 1945.

There were non-Japanese people who also suffered in Hiroshima. A large number of Koreans living in Hiroshima at that time were killed by the atomic bomb, as were exchange students from China and Southeast Asian countries. In addition, about 10 American prisoners of war died from the atomic bombing.

Memorial Monument for Hiroshima, City of Peace (Cenotaph for the A-bomb Victims)

Located in the center of the Peace Memorial Park, the Memorial Monument for Hiroshima, City of Peace is also called the "Cenotaph for the A-bomb Victims." This cenotaph was designed in the shape of an ancient Japanese clay burial house to keep the souls of those who perished in the atomic bombing out of the rain. The unveiling took place on August 6, 1952.

The former cenotaph had been made of reinforced concrete and in March 1985, the cenotaph was reconstructed by stones in the same size and shape as the original.

Under the cenotaph, there is a stone coffin in which a register of the names of atomic bomb victims who have died is dedicated. Every year new names, reported by Hiroshima City and other areas, are added to this register.

The front of the stone coffin reads, "Let All the Souls Here Rest in Peace; For We Shall Not Repeat The Evil." It means that all of us who are human beings pledge ourselves not to repeat such an evil that would again lead to a tragedy such as that of the atomic bombing of Hiroshima.

Cenotaph for the A-bomb Victims

Chapter 2

Testimony of Survivors

I Chanted Sutras Before the Ashes of the A-bomb Victims

by Fumie Enseki

An air-raid warning sounded during the night of August 5, 1945, and we all assembled at the Air Defense Headquarters at City Hall. I was a squad leader at the time, so that warning meant a busy night for me. When I climbed to the highest point of the roof of City Hall, I noticed black smoke rising from the Ube area of Yamaguchi Prefecture. I immediately descended to the basement to report this to Air Defense Department Chief Kubo. Then I began an all-night vigil.

The next morning, just after 7:00, I returned to my lodgings in Takaramachi, hoping for a few hour's sleep. I had just finished chanting sutras for my ancestors and lain down when I heard a terrific roar. Suddenly I realized I was in great pain. I was starting to lose consciousness. I thought I would die. But I found my arms could move, so I thrust them upwards with all my might and, seeing before me a patch of gray sky, struggled painfully to crawl out.

I thanked my ancestors that I was still alive. People covered with blood appeared all around me, looking hopelessly for some sort of refuge. Most were completely naked. Some were wearing what I assumed to be tatters of clothing, but when I looked closer I was shocked to find that the tatters were in fact hanging skin, burned and peeling off. What am I to say of these wretched figures? My pen is sadly inadequate to the task of describing them. I found a neighbor who was unable to stand. I helped her up and supported her as we walked toward Hijiyama Hill for refuge.

We crossed a bridge and on the other side were masses of injured people writhing in pain. I heard cries of "Water! Water!" "It hurts!" and "Kill me!". A school boy staggered about on broken glass and boards with protruding nails, looking as if he might die at any moment. His entire body was covered with burns and glass shards clung to his flesh; he cried out in anguish, "It hurts, it hurts." I went over to help him, but when I tried removing the glass fragments from his body, blood and bits of flesh came with them and he grimaced with pain. I said to him, "You must be in great pain," but through loud sobs he answered, "No, the pain doesn't bother me. Just please call my mother and father." There was absolutely nothing I could do for him.

All night long I gave out water to people. Someone asked me to chant a sutra for his grandmother, as she had just died. While I was chanting, a boy, who couldn't have been more than ten years old, called me 'Onee-chan.' (Pronounced 'Ohneh-chan,' this word means 'older sister.') "Thank you for the water, Onee-chan," he shouted, despite his great pain. "Your feet are bleeding, so take my shoes," and he threw his shoes to me. Looking down I saw that one of my feet was bare and dripping with blood. There was a sandal on the other one. Stopping the blood with my fingers, I put on the shoes. When I saw him the next morning, lying still as if in sleep, I saw he was dead. Crying out in anguish, I bowed my head to his noble heart. The sutras I chanted for him that night came directly from my soul.

During the night, soldiers from Ujina drove up in a truck. They stacked the injured on the bed of the truck, handling them as if they were logs or food sacks instead of humans. I asked one of the privates to treat them more gently, and he rebuked me sharply, explaining that there were far too many bodies to handle delicately. Then I saw that this hard-working soldier himself was covered with blood. I apologized to him. The soldier spoke to me more kindly. "There's blood coming from your back too, and pieces of glass are sticking out. You'd better lie down for a

Drawing by an A-bomb Survivor:
Taking care of survivors in the grounds of Hiroshima City Hall. Some
are near death.   (by Fumie Enseki)

while." I found out from Captain Takahashi, however, that the soldier died only six months later.

Staying up through that long night caused my feet to stiffen with fatigue. The next morning I began to worry about the staff from City Hall and decided to walk there through the burnt ruins to try to help. I saw countless naked and piteous corpses along the way. Chanting sutras the entire length of my journey I finally arrived and found Deputy Mayor Morishita and Mr. Nakamura from the Secretarial Division. I learned later that seven staff members had battled the fires like *samurai* and had managed, incredibly, to save three rooms.

Injured people crowded into the Family Registration Division, the Account Division and the other two rooms. The basement was filled with water and floating corpses. Someone told me cans of mandarin oranges were stored down there, so I waded through that horrible water to get them. I found some powdered milk there as well and distributed both to the survivors. Despite their terrible pain, they all accepted this nourishment gratefully and thanked me repeatedly for it. I finally lay down after midnight, but found that pain from the glass fragments in my back made sleep impossible. When I heard people call, "I want City Hall Onee-chan!" I forgot about sleep altogether and got up to help them.

The next day passed, and late that night a truck came by and delivered rice balls to us. People could only say, "This is a treasure, truly a treasure," as they gratefully accepted the food. I noticed a woman about to eat a rice ball with a fly stuck to it and tried to pick it off. But she scolded me, declaring that it was merely a sesame seed. As she ate she would take a bite, bow in thanks, and then take another, repeating the same ritual. "My son died of malnutrition. If only I could have let him eat his fill!" she mourned, crying over his memory.

Maggots began to appear in the wounds of the injured. Hungry children mistook them for rice, and I had to stop them from eating the maggots. Seeing these little ones in such a heart-rending state made the tears flow from my eyes.

One child said to me, "Onee-chan, your back is bleeding. You must be in pain, but still you helped us all night."

An elegant woman burned over her entire body, her hands clasped in prayer, told me between sobs that she had gold and silver and expensive jewels buried at such and such an address, and she would give them all to me if I would just save her life. Her misery impressed me deeply with the overriding sanctity of life itself. I tried to soothe her, explaining that I would care for her as best I could, not for money's sake, but from compassion. I tried to give her various things to eat, but her health deteriorated rapidly. She died the night of August 11.

The woman lying next to her relayed her message to me: "Thank you, City Hall Onee-chan, for taking care of me so well. I hope you live forever. Live for me too. I pray for your happiness." After saying this she died in peace. Two weeks later, the woman who relayed the message died as well. My sadness for them is so overwhelming it threatens to tear my heart apart.

Around 10:00 on the night of August 7, a girl about eight years old called desperately for me. "Grandma, Grandma!" she cried, for some reason mistaking me for her grandmother. She clung to me tightly when I went to her, murmuring her joy in finally finding me. Then I noticed that both her eyes were injured and that she had lost her sight. The child was in such misery I couldn't bear to look at her. I cried and cried as I hugged her to me. I simply held her close and remained silent, pretending for those ten minutes or so that we were truly granddaughter and grandmother. But then another pitiful voice cried out for me over and over, forcing me to call that I would come. Hearing my voice, the girl must have realized I was not her grandmother. Her anguish was such that she cried, "Kill me." Listening to that feeble voice repeatedly crying, "Kill me," many others began to cry, too. In my pity my tears also started again. At this she became even more hysterical, sobbing over and over the words, "Nanny isn't here. Nanny isn't here." When she stopped she told me that her throat was in pain, and asked me to give her some water. I gave her some milk, and she gulped it down thankfully, murmuring how good it tasted. Rations* of *conpeitō** and dry bread had been distributed and I gave her some of the candy. She devoured it. That girl breathed her last a week later. Just before she died she spoke her last words to me in a pained voice: "Onee-chan, thank you, thank you. I'll pray for your happiness in heaven." I will never forget her precious spirit. I still pray for the peace of her soul.

I also remember a boy about 10 years old with elegant white skin. Blood dripped from his side, which was nearly covered with burns. Maggots bred in his flesh, and often he would pluck them from his body to eat. His head too was so wounded that he probably couldn't discern what they actually were. He was so pitiful that it was difficult to look at him. "Grandmother,

Grandmother, give me water, water! It hurts so much; please take me home." When he first mistook me for his grandmother I looked at him in surprise; but when I saw that eyes were burned and sightless I understood. His condition was so heartbreaking I could not look at him directly. All I could do was to give him water. He often begged for it, and after drinking a little would say, "It's good, Grandmother. You'd better have some too," exactly as if I had this intimate connection with him. I cared for this child as best I could, but he soon died as well.

I believe it was in the middle of the night on the 8th when a man about 35 or 36 years old spoke to me in the Family Registration Division office of City Hall. "Miss, please help me. My wife and children are at home in the country, and I want to get back to them. But my legs are no good." I could see from the severe burns covering his whole body that he could not walk.

"I'm sure your wife and family will come to find you," I assured him.

"They said they would come to Hiroshima on the 6th, so they probably did. But I think I'll die before I can meet them. I want to see them just once more before I go, but my entire body is burned and my arms and legs hurt terribly. My friends proudly went to war for Japan and died. Now I'm reduced to this and I can do nothing but wait for death. I hate war, I despise it." By the end his voice had dropped so I could barely make out his words. He pleaded with me to help him, so I gave him water and he quieted down. But a few minutes later he called out for more water, now crying from the pain, his voice growing weaker and weaker. While on Hijiyama Hill I had heard someone say that giving burn victims too much water only hastens their death. I forced myself to deny his requests and moved on to help the other patients. Then, a woman about 32 years of age with a boy of about 12 appeared at the building, asking if she could look for her husband. She had brought a cart in which to carry him in case he was injured. I led her around to all the patients, hoping against hope that one might prove to be her husband.

Miraculously, they were none other than the wife and child the injured man so longed to see before he died. You see, they were afraid he was already dead, and he feared the same for them. When they finally found one another their joy was inexpressibly moving. All they could do was to hold each other and cry.

I thanked God for their reunion. As the man lay on his back in the cart carrying him away, his pain did not stop him from bowing politely to us until he was out of sight. I prayed that he might live until he reached home. The reason my hopes for him were so slim was that I had been watching many die with lesser injuries than his. I had heard that one could not recover from burns covering a third or more of the body. I prayed to God and Buddha to lessen the pain of these people and make them well. Each time I made a round of the patients, another had died. I was powerless to help them recover. All I could do was to pray for their spirits when they departed.

I also remember caring for a university student with a terrible case of tuberculosis. One day he tearfully confessed to me, "I'm a traitor to my country because I was too weak to fight as a soldier." From his throat to his stomach, his almost naked body was nothing but a huge, festering sore. At that time I never dreamed he would take his life, that his guilt would bring him to take a knife to his own throat. But late one night at around 1:30 a.m..... The woman who had lain next to him told me the story. "Yesterday he was shouting, 'Kill me! Kill me!' and seemed to be suffering terribly. When night came he told me of his plan and asked me not to tell anyone. Before he did it he requested, 'Tell City Hall Onee-chan that I thank her'." I wept miserably when I heard this. At that moment all I could feel was my hatred for war. Why, why did that young man have to die? I prayed for the repose of the soul of the youth who had died in agony, hating war.

One after another the ashes of cremated victims were brought in, and we placed them in the mayor's office and the mayor's meeting room on the second floor. These rooms were quickly filled to capacity. I made up my mind. I asked permission of Deputy Mayor Shibata to chant sutras and prayers for the souls of those victims. He agreed to this and left it to me, as there was no one else. I went to the unlighted room, by then pitch black. I chanted sutras continuously that night. Later, when relatives came to collect the ashes of their loved ones, I checked the name list and chanted sutras again before I delivered the ashes into their hands. About that time, a little boy came to collect the ashes of his family. He had lost both parents, his older brother, and his sister as well. Weeping miserably, he asked me to chant five sutras for each of them. I was oblivious to the passing of time as I offered up each chant, crying in sympathy with the boy. The look of him then is still burned into my eyes.

Tanka Poem

Small boy clasping four
Boxes of ashes to his chest.
Forgetting time,
I cry alongside him.

The ashes of various war victims were placed into pure white boxes and brought to the Mayor's office. We kept them there for 110 days, at which time they were removed to Zenpōji Temple in Koi. On April 27 of the following year, Colonel Tyer of GHQ* came to Hiroshima and brought those ashes back to City Hall. He made a color documentary film of me working on the third floor there. When he returned to America he took that film with him.

Praying for the peaceful repose of the departed souls.

Girl sobs for A-bombed Mother,
Father killed in battle.
Forgetting time, I cry with her.

In the wee hours
A youth pierces his throat
With a rusty needle.
How he hated war!

Wretched sight – a boy
Eating maggots swarming in his wounds,
Believing they were rice.

Five years ago, while I was undergoing tests at Funairi Hospital, an elderly gentleman approached one night asking me to hear his confession. For thirty-some years he had been undergoing treatment for physical injuries – his mental anguish, however, was even greater. He told me the story of his suffering.

"On August 6, badly burned and seeking refuge, I saw by the riverbank a woman of around 30 who was seriously injured and about to give birth. In great pain she was waving her arms wildly and calling, pleading for someone to help her. But I too was suffering, so I turned away from her to seek help for myself. I arrived at the first-aid center and, after receiving treatment, began to worry about the woman I had seen earlier. Two hours later I hurried back to the spot where I had seen her, but by this time both she and her baby were dead. The baby was a boy with a beautifully angelic face, and I hid my face in guilt. If only I had gone to them before, I might at least have saved the infant..... Knowing I abandoned them to their deaths, I have lived haunted by guilt ever since. I hope to God that someday you will write or tell my story." When I telephoned him two months later, I was told that he had died the day before. This stunned me, and I sadly chanted sutras for him that night. They came directly from my heart.

Three years ago I spoke with another woman also tremendously guilt-ridden over her experience that day. She telephoned me one day wanting to unburden herself. I will present her story now as she told it to me then.

"On August 6, while trying to flee the city, my three children and I sought refuge in an air-raid shelter*. It was small and crowded, so I decided to leave there to find a larger air-raid shelter. But the moment we entered the street, black rain began to fall. I immediately grabbed a pan lying nearby on the road and sheltered my youngest child with it. But she cried that it was too hot and pushed it away. I then held it over my middle child, but he also complained of the heat and pushed it away. Finally I covered my oldest child with it. Several months later, my two youngest children, who had both walked in the rain, vomited blood and died in agony. When I think of my stupidity and carelessness – I should have used anything, even the clothes I wore, to protect them – I am choked with remorse. That happened decades ago, but even now I suffer over it." She talked to me for two hours of this, weeping continuously. Then I told her of my own pain and tried my best to comfort her.

During that period there were a few men interested in marrying me, one of whom had been a military policeman. Although he strongly pressed for marriage, his parents in Tokyo refused because I was an A-bomb victim. His relatives, too, were unified in their opposition, and so it all came to nothing. I suffered great disappointment. Finally, however, a fifth man showed a strong interest in me. Captain Enseki pushed through his family's opposition and we were able to marry. But after marriage I experienced the heartache of miscarriage many times; each time, knowing that my A-bomb injuries had robbed my body of the ability to handle the strain of pregnancy, my sadness became unendurable.

I had many other terrible experiences and sometimes came close to committing suicide, but each time, as I approached the train tracks, I would hear those voices calling out to me, "I want you to live for me too." When those people appeared in my mind's eye, they silenced any thoughts of killing myself.

I saw some of my former colleagues at the City Employees 8·6 Meeting held during the 40th year after the bombing. Some told me that they had seen "Doi-san's (my maiden name) picture in the newspaper and on television" and were happy to learn that I was still alive. I, too, was delighted to find them still alive.

Today again the nameless ashes,
One following the next.
Unable to sleep,
I think of their families.

Crying and praying for the ashes,
This night too
My body is aching.

In the shadow of these
Hundreds of thousands of ashes
I chant sutras
And make my confessions.

Late at night an anguished voice calls
"City Hall Onee-chan!"
I run quickly to help him.

"In the next world,"
Said the boy,
"I will pray forever
For your happiness."

As he thanked me again and again,
The patient's labored breathing only
Reverberates in my ears.

When the ragged A-bomb survivors approached,
I saw their rags were skin.
Unable to look,
I bowed in prayer.

"Precious rice, precious rice!"
Sobbing while she eats,
The anguished mother bows in thanks,
And I feel pity.

That Day

by Setsuko Iwamoto

I was 13 and a second-year student at a girl's high school. I was exposed to the A-bomb explosion in our wooden school building 1.4 kilometers from the hypocenter.

In the spring of 1945 air raids in Tokyo were intensifying, so my sister, a third-grade pupil in national (elementary) school*, and I were sent away from Tokyo to my grandparents' house in Itsukaichi, a suburb just west of Hiroshima. Japan's war situation worsened, and the mainland was bombed day after day by American bombers. Nearly all our major cities were reduced to expanses of rubble. Hiroshima, to stop air-raid fires from spreading, began implementing a program of forced building demolition. Houses and other buildings were destroyed and removed to create open spaces for refuge and firebreaks to help the firefighters.

At the time, students in the upper grades of national and middle-level schools and above were mobilized. The slogan was "100 million in full production" (referring to Japan's population then of about 100 million), so we were working in factories and other workplaces.

My group was assigned to assist a group of adults in tearing down houses. On August 6, I was going to work in Tsurumi-chō. We were to meet at the school by 7:30 a.m. There we would receive our assignments and head for our work sites. A yellow air-raid warning sounded while I was on my way to school. After arriving at school, we all waited in our respective classrooms for the morning meeting to begin. After a while, the bell rang for

43

the morning meeting. Some quick students were already in the schoolyard. The slow ones were still in the classrooms on the second floor. I walked down the stairs and was waiting my turn to go out. But the exit was crowded. It looked like I would have a hard time getting out. Worrying that I would be late for the meeting if I waited, I passed by a first-grade classroom and headed for the west exit. As I did so, an intense golden flash struck me from ahead and to the right. Looking toward it and wondering what it might be, I was struck by a much more powerful bluish flash.

The next thing I knew, people all around me were crying out, "Mother, help me. Teacher, help me." I found myself trapped under the collapsed school building. I was sure a bomb had hit our school. I knew from our daily air-raid training that I had to hurry to get out of the building because fire would be coming soon and I would be burned alive. But despite having heard the voices calling for help, I have no memory of how I crawled out.

Somehow I escaped, and when I stood again on flat ground it seemed to be early evening. None of the buildings or trees that had stood there moments before could be seen. I was engulfed in an eerie silence and felt, for an instant, that I might be the only living thing on Earth. I will never forget that feeling.

I was brought to myself by cries and shouts. Looking around, I saw a group of people by the school gate. I approached and found that all of them were burned black over their entire bodies. The skin was sliding off their faces and arms, hanging in shreds and tatters. Their hair was dry and disheveled. Their clothes were torn, and they carried their hands up by their chests. It was impossible to recognize them from their faces. They were guessing each other's names by their *monpe** (work pants) and their voices. I quickly put my hands to my face and was relieved to find that the skin on my face had not peeled off. However, the uniform top and *monpe* I was wearing were torn to shreds. An embarrassing amount of bare skin was showing. My arms and legs were burned and peeling on the side from which I had received the flash. My air-raid hood* was missing, as were my emergency bag, my shoes, and the pin that had been in my hair. My body was so hot I thought it might be burning. My throat was parched, and my mouth and nose so full of dust I could hardly breathe.

My home economics teacher was burned over her entire body and in a frightful condition, but she shouted loudly, "Run to Ōkō National School. Run toward Hijiyama Hill*." As if her words had suddenly freed us from paralysis, a large group of us headed for Hijiyama Hill in a stream. On the way, we saw people clustered around fire cisterns. Some were drinking the inky black water or splashing it on their hot bodies. Others were plunging their heads in or climbing in completely.

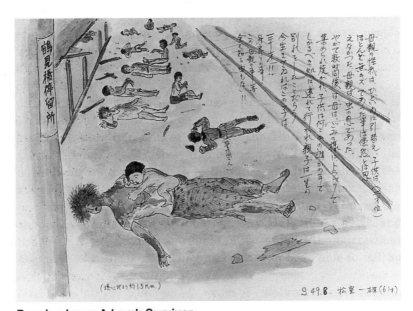

Drawing by an A-bomb Survivor:
A Child Clinging to its Dead Mother (Tsurumi Bridge)
(by Kazuo Matsumuro)

I fled barefoot over the rubble trying to avoid toppled electric poles and hanging wires. I saw crowds of people clustered around a place where water was spraying from a broken pipe. Someone was shouting, "If you're burned, don't drink. You'll die." A frantic mother was screaming, "Come help me! Save my trapped child!" Naked children ran around crying and searching for their parents. Soldiers burned bald except where their field caps had been were running around in complete confusion. Most were burned and peeling from their faces down to their waists. Everywhere I looked I saw the most horrible misery.

When I got to Hijiyama Bridge, I met a friend I used to walk to school with every morning. She invited me into the river to cool my burning body. I said, "Let's keep going to Hijiyama like the teacher said." I pulled her by the hand, but she and the person she was with left me and went down to the river. Crowds of people were already down in the river, and many others were streaming toward it. I saw my friend and her friend as I crossed the bridge, but that was the last time. To this day, I never heard what became of them.

I had just transferred from a school in Tokyo, so I didn't know Hiroshima very well. Along the way, I wandered and kept getting lost. At one point an older woman put some sort of oily stuff on my arms and legs. Eventually, I ended up at the Army Clothing Depot*.

Hundreds of people were already taking refuge in the Depot. I was laid down on an army blanket spread out on the concrete warehouse floor. Those consciousness enough to say their names and addresses received name tags, which were attached to their blankets near their heads. The tags were necessary because family members coming to find them would not be able to recognize their faces. My face was burned and so swollen I could hardly see. Maybe because I felt safe enough to relax, I suddenly found I could no longer move.

You might say we were getting treatment at the Depot, but the whole city was destroyed. Very little medicine was available. Many people were burned so badly you could see their white bones. Because of the heat, the tissue began to rot immediately. Flies were everywhere laying their eggs. Soon maggots were hatching out of white balls to crawl around in the wounds. I can still hear the screams of people in agony.

"Water. Please give me water!" They were given tiny sips from the spout of a kettle. Some whose mouths were too burned to drink got water from cloth soaked in water and wrung out over them. Only a few drops at a time got into their mouths, but that was the only way they could drink.

I was able to return home when my family finally found me on August 15. Even at home there was no medicine, so my grandmother put cucumber juice on me, with talcum powder on that to prevent heat rash. I have no idea where she heard about such treatment, but that was all they could do. Every morning the cloth on my burns was wet with blood and pus. I will never forget how much it hurt when she changed that cloth. What she did was effective, however, and a new, thin skin began forming over the burns. Then, I started losing my hair and my gums began to bleed. I had diarrhea and felt terrible. In other words, I began to show the symptoms of what we called "A-bomb disease."

The night before the bombing I had found a small pimple on my head when I washed my hair. It was so small I had forgotten it entirely, but now it grew bigger and bigger, until it created a bald spot about 5 or 6 centimeters across that was festering. Blood and pus flowed from it constantly, and the back of my head and pillow were always damp. It was disgusting. My grandmother said it smelled as bad as the Army Clothing Depot. We didn't know what to do, so we crumpled and salted the leaves of a herb called *dokudami* (saururaceae), and every day we changed the poultice several times. My grandmother said that no matter how much she washed the pillowcase, she could never completely remove the stains.

In September, a friend of my grandfather's saw the sore on my head and said, "We should lance this." He sharpened my grand-father's razor and, without any sort of antiseptic, he just cut it. My head was over a washbasin, and enough blood and pus came out to fill a large rice bowl. Because the flesh there was so rotten, I didn't feel any pain. We continued to put *dokudami* on it, and after that it healed quickly.

All we had was folk medicine. I have a feeling that I was saved because I returned to my house, drank plenty of water, then got that infection on my scalp and had it cut and drained. Somehow, I think the radiation that got into my body the day of the bombing was drained out. In any case, I believe I was very lucky.

When I got back to my house on August 15, the mother of the girl I used to walk to school with and met at Hijiyama Bridge came over to see if I knew where she might be. I said I left her at the bridge, but I did not say anything about her and her friend going down to the river. Every day after that, her mother would come over to report, "Today, I searched such and such a place but I couldn't find her." Why hadn't I pulled harder on their hands when we met at the bridge? Why hadn't I tried harder to make them cross the bridge with me? More than fifty years later I still struggle with this question.

One day in fall, an article appeared in the paper saying that students were to bring their chopsticks and gather at their schools to collect bones from the burned-out ruins. When I arrived, all that was left of my school was the *Hōanden* (shrine)* to the right of the front gate and the fireproof east-west wall of the building.

That day I had come down the stairs and gone first to the crowded exit. Now that area was full of bones waiting for me. If I had stood there another minute waiting my turn to leave, someone would have been picking up my bones. This thought filled me with a deep, powerful emotion. I left no bone ungathered.

We searched the school grounds and the dormitory. We found

innumerable bones with hair or partially burned flesh still clinging to them, and we lined all the bones up on burned sheets of tin roofing. We took them to the ruins of Jisenji Temple, which was where the Atomic Bomb Memorial Mound stands today in Peace Memorial Park. Other bones and decomposed flesh brought in from around the city were piled up like a mountain and covered with straw mats.

One day when the autumn sun was still very hot, a memorial service was held for the victims in Hiroshima. Many seeking water in the rivers lost strength and simply floated away without a trace. That one instantaneous event killed tens of thousands of people. The vast majority of students in my class died on August 6 or shortly thereafter. Many who did manage to survive suffered and eventually died from the aftereffects.

I saw misery that day that I cannot believe was of this world. The voices of those war victims will never be heard. As a survivor, it is my mission to speak on their behalf and tell their story to the next generation.

We Never Found Our Daughter's Bones

by Kikue Komatsu

Forty-five years have passed, and still pain tightens around my chest when I bring up those memories. The atomic bombing was the most immense, single catastrophe ever visited on this Earth. August 6, 1945, started off beautifully cloudless and calm. Then, out of the blue we were attacked by a flash, heat rays, and radiation. All of central Hiroshima was engulfed in savage fires, growing into an immense conflagration, transforming people into figures more ghostly and monstrous than human.

At the time our house was in Minami-misasachō, about 1.7 kilometers from the hypocenter. My husband and I lived there with our 17-year-old daughter, who was working at the Hiroshima Central Telephone Office. Before she left for her 2 p.m. shift on August 5, I recall her saying, "Mother, there will probably be a huge air raid on the seventh or eighth, so please be very careful!" Then she walked out of the house with a spring in her step. I did not ordinarily see her off to work, but that day I stood in the doorway and watched until she disappeared from sight.

That night the roar of the planes overhead battled with the din of the air-raid warnings and sporadic announcements from military headquarters. I was filled with foreboding. The following morning, too, planes sounded overhead, and I felt intuitively that Hiroshima was about to be bombed. But the yellow air-raid warning was finally lifted, and I remember thinking, "Well, we're all right for now." At 7:00 a.m. my husband left for his job at a munitions factory in Kabe. Waiting for my daughter to return from work I went to the kitchen to prepare her breakfast. Just then a voice came on the radio to announce another yellow air-raid warning. I thought, "What? Again?" but after a few minutes it was lifted. I was about to go out to the back of the house when suddenly I heard a tremendous roar. Then, I lost consciousness.

When I came to, I found myself trapped under the ruins of our house. I was in pitch darkness. A large beam pressed painfully into my shoulder, pinning me down. It seemed hopeless, and I tried over and over to prepare myself for death. Yet I kept struggling with all my might to free myself. Eventually, by the grace of God, a crack of light appeared in the darkness. I fought my way toward it and somehow managed to crawl from the house.

Once free of the debris, I heard other people trapped under their houses. Their imploring voices tore at me but, as blood poured from my wounded feet, I knew I lacked the strength to help them. It was hell on earth. Dragging my feet, I tried to flee, but my body failed me. I fell, but fear for my daughter gave me new strength. I somehow got up and dragged myself down the road.

To my left and right ghost-like people lay in the street; most seemed dead. I feared my daughter might have died too. I was overcome with dread. I happened to meet my husband, who, fortunately, had returned safely. We embraced tearfully. We were utterly distraught over our daughter, but what could we do? By evening Hiroshima City was one great sea of flame.

We waited for daybreak, then set off toward the telephone office where she worked. By now I was oblivious to the pain in my feet. The road was covered with corpses. Those still alive cried out miserably for water, but there was no water nearby. We could do nothing for them. We put our hands together in prayer to ask their forgiveness and continued our journey. When we finally arrived at my daughter's building, all we saw was a stack

Drawing by an A-bomb Survivor:
People crowding around a fire cistern. (Aioi Bridge vicinity)
(by Kikue Komatsu)

of bodies burnt past recognition.

Heartbroken, my husband and I tried to return home, but we continually lost our way. When we finally reached what we thought was our neighborhood, we were panting with exhaustion. Not far away, groups of floating corpses bumped against each other like rafts on the Motoyasu, Honkawa, and Tenmagawa Rivers.

In spite of what we had seen, my husband and I clung to a slim hope that our daughter had been walking home when caught by the bomb, so we continued to search for her every day. These are cruel memories. A week later, we learned what had become of her. At the time of the explosion, she and the other workers were on the balcony for roll call. Outside the building, their bodies would have borne the full impact of the blast and heat. No remains of our daughter were ever found.

It has now been forty-five years of constant suffering. I cry, but somehow the tears are never spent. When I think of that tragedy, I know that the A-bomb catastrophe was a product of war. Japan was the first to be A-bombed, but my deepest wish is that the horror endured by Hiroshima and Nagasaki be conveyed to the far corners of this world. To treasure human love and to build world peace: does not this give joy and meaning to life? As a witness and survivor of the A-bomb, I want to communicate the dire reality of that experience and share my story with others for as long as I live. Though every country is different, I truly believe the world is one. I join hands with the other survivors of Hiroshima and Nagasaki and beg all the nations of the world to stop building those nuclear weapons that threaten someday to exterminate all humankind.

Fifty years from now, the eyewitness survivors will probably be gone. Thus, I want to see an A-bomb Survivor Support Law passed as soon as possible. Such a law would be a way for the country to express its condolences and sympathy – for those who died in agony and for those still suffering today. We cannot wait any longer. Not much time remains for me, but I wanted to take this opportunity to ask you all for your support.

I have written this account from a heart overflowing with emotion.

Note : This testimony is presented as it was written in 1987. On December 9, 1994, the Law concerning Support for Those Exposed to the Atomic Bomb was enacted. However, because the law does not include the "national compensation" and "individual condolences for the dead" that survivors have been demanding, survivor groups and other organizations continue to press for a *hibakusha* support law that specifies national compensation.

Between Auschwitz and Hiroshima

by Seikō Komatsu

I was nine years old, a fourth grader in elementary school (called national elementary school then), when the atomic bomb fell on Hiroshima.

I experienced the explosion in our house, located directly behind the National Railway's Nishi-Hiroshima Station (Koi Station at the time) on the Sanyō Line, only 2.5 kilometers from the hypocenter.

The Schoolchildren Evacuation Reinforcement Guidelines* were decided in March 1945. From April to July, 1945, national school pupils from the third to sixth grades in Hiroshima City were evacuated in groups to temples and community halls in seven counties: Saeki, Asa, Yamagata, Takada, Futami, Sera, and Hiba. I should have been one of the children safely evacuated. But my parents, however, had both died when I was a year old, and my grandparents, who had raised me since then, did not want me separated from them. Ironically, their love for their grandchild brought him unhappy consequences.

On the morning of August 6 I awoke at around 6:00, and with my grandmother boarded a Hiroden Railway Miyajima Line tramcar. We got off four stops later at Kusatsu Station, approximately 4.5 kilometers from the hypocenter. My grandmother was regularly commuting to a clinic in that area to receive treatment for a nerve problem in her foot, and she used to take me with her. That day four or five patients were ahead of her, and I was too hungry and impatient to wait. I took the train home alone to eat breakfast.

Just after I had grumbled my way through a meal of inferior boiled barley, an intense red flash lit up the window glass, followed by a tremendous roar! I was thrown about five meters and landed violently on the tatami floor. In my mind, all was darkness, and I had no idea what had happened. After a while I came to myself and stood up. Looking around, I saw the window glass shattered to tiny splinters and the chest and dish cupboards fallen over. A shard of glass pierced my left knee and I was bleeding. Both my elbows were burned.

Something hard had fallen from the ceiling on my grandfather's head, leaving a gaping wound about five centimeters long. Fortunately, we had some yellow medicinal powder for emergencies, and he sprinkled this on his gash. Then he grabbed my hand and took me to an air-raid shelter located at the foot of a mountain some distance west of us. People filed past the shelter, many whose deep burns indicated they had been exposed near the hypocenter. Miserably, they trudged on, seeking refuge in the countryside.

In a little while, a middle-aged woman entered our shelter pulling a younger woman by the hand. At first glance I thought the young woman must be a ghost – her deathly features, the hair standing straight up on her head, the ragged and torn clothes. Severe burns spread from her face to her chest and arms. Her skin dangled from her, exposing ripped, red flesh. Drops of oil stood out on her darkened, swelling skin. The woman was truly a hideous sight.

There was no medication in our shelter. At the time, mercurochrome was the main treatment for wounds and injuries; most types of lesions were routinely painted bright red with this medicine. I wondered what could possibly be done for this woman. But suddenly the older woman picked up a small basin from the corner of the shelter and proceeded to urinate in it. She then soaked some torn rags in the urine and diligently set about washing the younger woman's wounds with the ammonia from her body. I can still vividly recall that scene.

Later, black rain began falling heavily over the northwest area of the city. That mixture of dirt and dust containing terrible radioactivity came down for nearly two hours. It finally stopped just before noon, at which time my grandfather led me by the hand to our home behind Nishi-Hiroshima Station.

Ours was a two-story wooden house standing on a seven-meter stone wall rising out of flat rice paddies. Completely unsheltered, it bore the full force of both the heat ray and blast. The rear of my house facing the epicenter had burst into flame. It appeared that the fire had burned for some time, until doused by the black rain. The blast itself had caused half of the second floor to collapse.

My grandmother, meanwhile, had been searching for us des-

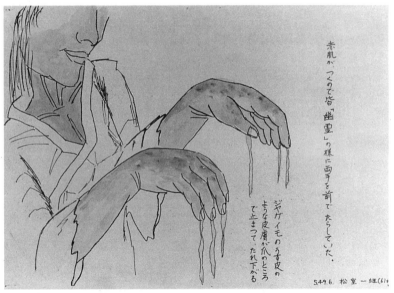

Drawing by an A-bomb Survivor:
This woman's skin is peeling and hanging from her fingers
(by Kazuo Matsumuro)

perately, walking the full two kilometers from Kusatsu back home in the black rain. When we got home around noon, we found her sitting on the floor, dazed and completely soaked, murmuring, "The rain hurt, it hurt so much I couldn't bear it...." She died in September of the next year.

People were dying one after another, and there was no place for cremating the corpses. The Report to the United Nations by Hiroshima and Nagasaki Cities estimated that 140,000 people died in the five-month interval between August and December 1945.

The nearby school sports field became a cremation site. I remember people digging huge trenches in the dirt, throwing the bodies inside, and burning them with oil fires. Many bodies were cremated this way. Some time later our desperation for food led us to plant sweet potatoes in this field. One day, while working the soil there, I felt my hoe catch on something. When I lifted the hoe a tangle of long, black hair was hanging from it – a woman's hair. Looking closer, I noticed flesh still clinging to it. Even now I shiver at this memory. We also found combs, fountain pens, and many other personal belongings as we tilled the area. At harvest time we fortunately got a large crop. Saying, "Delicious, delicious," we ate our fill.

My grandmother was one of those that got no proper cremation. Downstream from us on the Ohta River, there was an open area at the foot of the Asahi Bridge. We dug a trench there, stacked firewood in it, and laid her body on top. Then we doused it with oil and set it afire.

The following day I returned to this spot with my uncle to collect my grandmother's ashes. (He had been recently discharged from the military. He later fell ill with radiation sickness, vomited blood and died.) The bones of her windpipe had turned pure yellow and were as dry and fragile as a pumice stone. I thought it must have been from breathing radiation.

Life was very hard after the A-bomb dropped. Food, clothing and shelter are necessities of life, and we especially lacked food.

Many people said that nothing would grow in Hiroshima for 75 years, but as early as October, horseweed, mugwort and canna began to spring up and flower. If plants are able to grow, we reasoned, maybe humans will survive as well.

I remember walking around the city picking horseweed and mugwort to take home and mix into our gruel along with a few grains of rice. We had neither soy sauce, soybean paste, or sugar to use as flavorings. Our only seasoning was salt water obtained from the Ohta River. We would carry buckets and rope to the Asahi Bridge, tie them together, and lower the buckets into the current to get sea water. We hauled this home and stored it in a tall glass bottle to use for seasoning. We also heated it and sipped it as broth, but it tasted like what it was – sea water.

Eba is a district in the southern part of the city. Eba dumplings were made of horseweed and wild mugwort. To stave off hunger, people lined up and paid money for them. There was a limit of ten per person.

Right now, if someone brought me one of those dumplings, I probably would be unable to eat it. I would throw it away. In ordinary life, those balls of weeds would be considered inedible.

I suffered from malnutrition during that period. My arms and legs became extremely thin and my ribs showed clearly. I could get a good hold on them with my fingers. My distended abdomen and swollen face gave me the classic look of malnutrition. Needing some source of vitamins and calcium, I was forced to search the city for locusts and grasshoppers, which I later fried in a pan and ate.

We lacked clothes too. My student uniform was ragged and worn, but I had no choice but to continue wearing it.

As for shelter, on rainy days we had to put up umbrellas in the house exactly as if we were outside.

My grandfather died two years after the atomic bomb dropped, and I was sent off to live with an uncle in Ōsaka. The latent effects I had feared so much now came to pass. Since that onset during my first year of junior school, my life has been full of suffering and pain.

I became so weak it seemed as if weights were attached to my feet. Day after day I vomited, unable to take food. I could tolerate only noodles or thin rice gruel, and soon developed jaundice. Sent to the hospital for two months, I contracted hepatitis and my condition only worsened. At night my chest hurt terribly. Then I contracted emphysema with complications. Even now I suffer from impaired liver functioning and emphysema.

While I was working at the Hiroshima Peace Memorial Museum (often known as the Atomic Bomb Museum) at the end of 1983, I happened to read an article in the American magazine, *Science*. This article, written by Dr. Carl Sagan with a group of American scientists, brought back powerfully the horrible feelings of 1945. The article concerned a phenomenon called nuclear winter. According to these scientists, after a nuclear war the massive amounts of dirt and smoke generated by the explosions and the accompanying fires would block most of the sun's rays, resulting in a drastic cooling of the Earth's temperatures. Even in summer temperatures might drop below freezing. And even if the targets of a nuclear war all lay in the northern hemisphere, the southern hemisphere would be affected as well. The article concluded with a horrifying scenario: in the event of mutual nuclear attacks utilizing 5,000 to 10,000 megatons of destructive power, assuming half the human race survived this onslaught, they would be faced with ruinous climatic and environmental conditions and eventually fade into extinction, along with most other surviving creatures. By now, fortunately or unfortunately, many people know of this terrible danger.

Reading that article reminded me of the morning the atomic bomb was dropped, when my grandfather was pulling me by the hand to the closest air-raid shelter. It had been a completely cloudless, brilliantly sunny morning, hot enough to sweat sitting still. I had put on shorts and a short-sleeved shirt, and was still wearing these when I fled up the hillside path. That walk, though barely one kilometer, felt excruciatingly long to me. When I looked up, the sky was heavy with clouds. Shivering with cold on that walk was the memory that article had awakened for me. The summer sun never reappeared for us that day.

I experienced cold in summer from a single atomic explosion. What would come from a barrage of today's missiles, so incomparably more destructive than the atomic bombs used in 1945? That day, the chill crawling over my skin revealed the truth about nuclear winter. And now, whenever I relate my A-bomb experiences, I always tell of the cold that hit me on the hillside.

These are my words to the children of the computer generation. "When you play video games, you sometimes make mistakes, don't you? In the same way, the danger exists that someone will make a mistake with a button which controls the firing of nuclear weapons. As long as those weapons exist, we never know when we ourselves might experience a nuclear winter."

In August 1984, I had the opportunity as an A-bomb witness to visit the first Hiroshima-Nagasaki A-bomb Photo Exhibit held in Poland. During World War II, the Jewish people were persecuted viciously by the Nazis, and many were taken to the largest of the death camps, Auschwitz-Birkenau. The physically able were forced to do hard labor. The others were stripped of their clothes on the pretext that they were to take a shower; then they were marched into ghastly shower halls to be ruthlessly exterminated by poisonous Zyklon B gas. Women's heads were shaved, and some 750 kilograms of their hair was woven into clothes linings, blankets, and carpets.

Anyone who resisted the Nazis' orders was quickly taken out and shot. Exhibited in the Auschwitz Museum is the "Wall of Death." Starting with the murder of forty Poles by firing squad in November of 1940, this wall was the backdrop of more than 200,000 shooting deaths during the course of the war. It is displayed exactly as it was then.

I paid a courtesy call to Mr. Andrzej Telka, Mayor of Auschwitz, who told me that about 4,000,000 people were murdered in Poland for four years.

In front of an audience of about 300 Breslau townspeople, I told of my A-bomb experiences and tried to communicate the "Spirit of Hiroshima," the desire for the realization of lasting peace. I related my feelings about war: "When one thinks deeply about wars between nations, one quickly realizes that wars are at bottom nothing but emotional conflicts operating on the same principles as personal quarrels. I am striving to be the type of person who, even when arguing, considers the other's point of view in order to better understand my opponent's pain." After my talk, a middle-aged man who had lost both his parents to the gas chambers of Auschwitz came to speak with me. He gave me flowers and words of encouragement.

Although the slaughter by the Nazis and the atomic bombings of Japan were different events, both were grisly holocausts bringing unspeakable pain to their victims. The people I met at this conference had deep understanding and empathy with the plight of Hiroshima. We may be different in race, but we are all human beings. No human exists who does not want peace. In order to preserve the existence and dignity of the human race, we must cease our preoccupation with racial and national distinctions. We must all strive to conquer the invisible evil. For the sake of eternal peace, for the sake of humankind....

In the town of Auschwitz-Birkenau, small bones were scattered here and there, recalling the horror of those times. We must abolish nuclear weapons and reject war. Auschwitz is still etched on my mind.

My A-bomb Experience and the "Spirit of Hiroshima"

by Miyoko Matsubara

August 6, 1945 – 8:15 a.m.

I was exposed to the bomb while cleaning up debris from building demolition work in accordance with the Student Mobilization Ordinance*. I was in the first year at a Girls' High School, and the job site was Tsurumi-chō, 1.5 kilometers southeast of the hypocenter.

There were about 500 of us first-and second-year students at the site, as well as eleven of our teachers. We had been ordered to gather at the foot of Hijiyama Bridge by 7:30 a.m. At 7:09, a yellow air-raid warning suddenly sounded, and we all sought cover in shacks and other shelters. Soon, however, at 7:31, the all clear sounded, and we hurried on to our meeting place.

As we walked from Hijiyama Bridge to the work site under that cloudless, midsummer sky, we felt joyfully released from the tension of those eery air-raid warning sirens screaming out one after another. The hills and rivers glittered beautifully in the freshness of the morning. Passing Hijiyama Bridge and arriving at the Tsurumi-chō site, we found a small hut. There we left our air-raid hats and first-aid kits containing our lunch boxes and medicine, then set to work. The purpose of demolishing houses was to create open areas that would prevent the spread of fire in case of an attack.

The groups that had been summoned to this particular site quickly assembled, and we students from the lower grades of junior high and girls' high schools found ourselves working alongside members of the National Volunteer Corps* from surrounding neighborhoods. The Student Mobilization Ordinance was issued because of the labor shortage. It required students in the upper grades of national (elementary) school and middle-level schools (junior high, girls' high {or secondary} schools, and vocational schools) and above to engage in work for the war.

Therefore, students went to factories and made military supplies or munitions. Older students replaced adults in factories, companies, and farm fields. Younger students like us helped by cleaning up the debris from building demolition.

Vast numbers of students were mobilized for labor in Japan at that time. In March of 1945 we numbered 3,156,000, about 70% of the total number of eligible students. Except in rare cases, all classes were suspended; education in Japan, at least for a time, was at a standstill.

Hard at work, we spent our time gathering broken rooftiles, lumber, and nails, and piling them in baskets. I remember how four or five of us would lift these baskets and spiritedly call out, "One...two, one...two!" as we hauled them over to the designated spot.

Then it happened. One of my good friends, Takiko Funaoka, suddenly shouted, "I hear a B-29!" The yellow air-raid warning had just been lifted so I thought it couldn't be true, but I looked up at the sky nonetheless. Soon I spotted the white trail, which I followed until I could barely make out the outline of a plane headed northwest. Continuing to stare, I thought I saw a light that seemed both bluish white and orange. I quickly dropped to the ground. At the same moment, I heard a roar so deafening it seemed to shake the very foundations of the Earth. The force of the blast was tremendous, and I instantly thought the bomb must have fallen directly on me. I'm not sure how much time went by, but when I regained consciousness, I was in pitch darkness. The air was so clogged with dirt it was impossible to see. Neither Takiko nor the other two members of my team were near me. Apparently they had been tossed away by the blast.

The dust near the ground gradually cleared, and soon I was able to see. I stood up and gazed around in utter shock and amazement. My shirt was originally so white my mother was afraid it could be seen from a plane, so a few days earlier she had spent all day dying it a safer purple. The heat ray burned my *monpe* (baggy work pants). Only the cloth around my chest and back remained, and it was in tatters. I stood there in my dust-darkened undershirt and underpants. The tops of my feet were so burnt and swollen I thought they would burst. I hurriedly took my shoes off and threw them away.

That was when I realized that my hands, arms, legs and face – more than a third of my body – were severely burned. The burns were so severe my skin had swollen and was peeling off like slippery cellophane strips, exposing the bright red flesh underneath. The skin of my fingers and arms dangled here and there like rags. It was a sickly yellow flecked red with fresh blood. Terrified by my injuries, I was suddenly seized by the desire to get back to my family. I ran off, forgetting completely the heat and the pain, heading for where I might find people, falling and crawling in the dark over the rubble, desperate to get home.

After a while I thought I saw a clearing a little up ahead of me and, hurrying on, I finally reached the foot of a bridge. I was astonished at the number of wounded gathered on the banks seeking refuge – young people, old people, their clothes burned off their bodies by the heat rays, their faces blackened by dirt, blood pouring from their wounds. Some were charred completely black; only their white teeth seemed visible. Many walked or ran along as if possessed, the flesh of their faces horribly exposed. All emerged from that darkness in search of cool water; they hovered near the water below the bridge like ghosts. The river was blanketed by black smoke and haze. A huge choir of voices raised a chanting drone that sounded like the rumbling of the sea. Raising their arms to the heavens, the people plunged their pain-contorted faces into the water again and again.

Unbearably hot, I moved toward the water as if sucked in.

Someone approached and said in a thin, weak voice, "Aren't you Matsubara?" At first I had no idea who it was. The swollen and splitting burnt skin over her whole face left it a formless mass. Her lower lip in particular had swollen up so huge it was hard to tell exactly where her jaw ended and her neck began. And her eyes, once so pretty and bright, were now lost somewhere in misshapen folds of flesh. She was a friend from my class. Her grotesque transformation astounded me; I found it too painful to look at her directly. Still, in the midst of this hell I was over-joyed to meet a friend. For the first time since the explosion I found myself able to think calmly. I realized now that I had not been singled out, that everyone had been attacked and also real-ized the enormity of the damage all around me.

I stood still in the river, trying to gather strength by urging myself over and over to be strong. Then I began moving around, hoping to find other classmates somewhere in the crowds of peo-ple. But everything was in such a state of turmoil it was almost impossible to recognize anyone.

I saw then that flames were licking up high in the area from which I had just come. Fearing that in that spot we'd either be bombed by another enemy plane or succumb to the fires, I turned to that friend and urged her to get out of the water. Helping each other along, we somehow managed to crawl up onto the bank. While crossing the bridge, we passed people walking to and fro, aimless, like sleepwalkers. There were even people walking back toward the burning city. Continuing fur-ther, we arrived at a junction: turning right would take us to my house, going left would take us to our school.

We singlemindedly set out on the road to our school. On the way I noticed the streetcar wires of the Hijiyama Line mangled and knocked to the ground. Roadside trees reduced to bare trunks had toppled over, exposing their roots. Broken branches and leaves were scattered everywhere. People seeking water had dipped their heads into household fire-prevention water tanks and had simply died there. Walking further up Hijiyama

Drawing by an A-bomb Survivor:
A girl who breathed her last with no one to help her (Enkōgawa River)
(by Masato Yamashita)

Hill, I saw old men, women, and students simply sprawled along the road where they had come to the end of their strength. In some places their blood ran into the street, dyeing it a sickly reddish-black.

We came across a woman who had apparently escaped from her burning house and was now trying to run back in. A man held her tightly to prevent her, but she struggled violently, as if crazed, crying and screaming at him, "Let me go! My little boy...!" I couldn't believe such things could happen on this earth; it was truly a living hell.

We continued to run, fleeing as if some horrible thing were chasing us, and we finally reached the foot of another bridge. I think now it must have been Kōjin Bridge. There, Michiko told me she wanted to go to the East Drill Grounds. I, however, wanted to get back to school, and so, just before the bridge, we parted company. It was a terribly painful goodbye. Usually so strong and cheerful, Michiko just stood silent for a while, big teardrops running down her burned, distorted face. That this was our final parting....

After leaving Michiko, I hurried back to school. Passing through the narrow streets of Danbara, I noticed that many of the stores and houses were tilted askew. Fragments of glass doors lay shattered on the streets along with wooden doors, ceilings, shelves – all flung around randomly. With no place to set my feet, I was forced to make my way by squeezing along the edge of the road.

Finally, I made it to my school, the Hiroshima Girls' School of Commerce. From the road I could see that most of the school building had collapsed. Only the bathrooms and assembly hall remained recognizable. Unable to make myself enter the gate, I simply stood where I was awhile. When I regained my composure I kept walking.

Soon I reached the vicinity of my old primary school, Ōkō National Elementary School. Unable to struggle further against the heat and pain, I collapsed under the eaves of the Mizoguchis' house in front of the school, hoping someone would happen along and help me. Luck was with me. Mrs. Akino Hamamura from Kitaōkō passed by almost right away. She was going into the city to find out what had happened to her child, and she carried me on her back all the way to my house.

No one was home, so my neighbors used a broken door as a stretcher and carried me back to Ōkō National Elementary School, an emergency relief station. I received treatment there.

I'm not sure how many days had passed since the bombing when my temperature suddenly shot up to nearly 40 degrees. My stools were bloody, my gums bled, and my hair began falling out, leaving me half-bald. This went on for about ten days, and at one point led me so close to death I drifted off into unconsciousness. When I regained consciousness I was surrounded by neighbors solicitously watching over me. I felt anew my good fortune in having been allowed to live. I had come so close to death, but in eight months I was nearly completely recovered.

My main worry was what the burns had done to my face. I kept begging my mother, "Let me see a mirror," but she would never give me one. One day, when I was once again able to walk, I stole a glimpse of myself in the mirror. I was so aghast at my reflection I couldn't even make a sound. The face before me was hideously swollen, utterly transformed from the one my mother had given me. I looked like a red demon; the area around my eyes had wrinkled like a rotten tomato. I had no eyebrows. Realizing that this reflection was truly my own face, I burst out in misery and could not stop the tears. Whenever I was left alone, I sobbed without end, thinking, "If only my mother had given me better treatment,..." or "If only there had been no war, I wouldn't look like this."

My mother lamented with me, saying, "If only the bomb had gotten me instead. I'm older and don't have so much ahead of me. War is hateful." And when I writhed in agony she cried by my side, murmuring, "It would have been better if it had killed you then and there." I hovered between life and death for some time. My mother traded her best kimonos for food, then took the food to the physician in exchange for my injections. I often thought of my mother's hardships, and gradually came to the decision that I could not bring her any more suffering than she had already endured. I willed myself to become strong, and I pledged never again to cry when she was near.

When I returned to school after my eight months of recuperation, the 270 members of our student body had been reduced to about fifty. Though I had suffered the atomic bombing, I did not intend to be treated like a fool, so I studied very hard. Still, the horrible keloids on my face kept me from finding work after graduation. And men disliked marring A-bombed women.

I had gradually given up on the idea of receiving any substantial medical help, but eight years after the bombing, at age 20, I found myself in Ōsaka where I eventually underwent more than ten operations over a seven-month period. These operations were quite successful and, as a result, I was able to open and close my dysfunctional eyelid and to straighten out my crooked fingers. The results brought me pure elation, and I am filled with gratitude toward those people who reached out with warm, loving hands and softly stroked that eyelid that wouldn't shut.

I returned to Hiroshima wishing to express this gratitude in some way.

Just at that time, Reverend Kiyoshi Tanimoto of Nagarekawa (Christian) Church, who had given me the opportunity to have the operation, was establishing a home for blind children. The home took in 30 children with few relatives and little happiness in their lives. For eight years I was a member of the nursing staff at that home. That experience in community service helped me finally find meaning in my life. From then on, I began to think deeply about the atomic bomb. I realized that it is human beings who make war and atomic bombs. So unless human beings learn to hate war and nuclear weapons, protest evil, and raise their voices for the abolition of nuclear weapons, we will end up repeating the same evil. I resolved to devote my life to the struggle for the abolition of nuclear weapons.

After that, I worked at the Hiroshima Peace Culture Foundation for 27 years. Since retiring from the Foundation, I have traveled overseas twice each year to tell my A-bomb experience to foreign audiences. Recently, I have been communicating with people overseas over the Internet.

I still tell my A-bomb experience to young people who visit Hiroshima. When I do, I always include an apology for the actions of the Japanese military in Asia, but I will never think of the atomic bombing as a simple act of war. When those bombs destroyed Hiroshima and Nagasaki, the human race opened the door to the nuclear age, an age of potential extinction. Worldwide, we still have more than enough nuclear weapons to kill every creature on Earth many times over. If nuclear weapons are used again, the human race will be annihilated. There will be no winners or losers, no perpetrators or victims, only massive destruction. The human race must learn from Hiroshima and Nagasaki a lesson essential for our continued survival.

Now India and Pakistan have nuclear weapons. As we begin sliding down the foolish path toward nuclear proliferation, our only glimmer of hope is the policy of nuclear disarmament recently announced by Great Britain. Yet even England has no intention to abandon its nuclear weapons.

We stand at a crossroads. Will we increase the number of nuclear powers? Or will the five official nuclear powers make serious efforts toward nuclear disarmament and the abolition of nuclear weapons? We have to find a way. As long as we have nuclear weapons, there will never be world peace. Nuclear weapons and the human race cannot coexist indefinitely. As long as I live, I will continue, until the last nuclear weapon has been dismantled, appealing from Hiroshima on behalf of those who died. This year more than last. Next year more than this. I will speak with the words of an A-bomb survivor that the world might advance, even little by little, toward the abolition of nuclear weapons.

I Couldn't Press the Shutter in Hell

by Yoshito Matsushige

An air-raid warning siren awakened me not long after midnight, in the early morning of August 6. American B-29 bombers were flying over us day and night then, keeping me at such a pitch of fatigue that I often felt I'd rather die where I was than have to get up again at night. And yet, the eerie scream of that siren never failed to rouse me in fear for my life.

At the time, I was a photographer for the *Chūgoku Shimbun* (Hiroshima's local newspaper), but whenever the sirens sounded I was assigned to the news department of the Hiroshima Imperial Headquarters. As usual, after the siren went off that night, I quickly rode to headquarters without using the light on my bicycle. The all clear sounded at 2:00 a.m., and I lay down on the wooden bench at the office and drifted off to sleep. When I awoke, a perfectly clear morning greeted my eyes. The sun was shining so brilliantly it shocked me to remember we were still at war. The morning feigned peace; no one had any idea that a mere hour later an atomic bomb would be dropped and reduce the entire city to ashes, stealing away tens of thousands of lives.

It was too early to go straight to the newspaper office, so I returned to my home in Midorimachi (South Hiroshima), about four kilometers from the Imperial Headquarters and 2.7 kilometers from the hypocenter. That decision saved my life, for both the headquarters and the newspaper building stood about one kilometer from the hypocenter.

I had just finished breakfast. My underwear was out on the

clothesline where I had hung them because I had gotten them rather sweaty. I was standing up to get them when, suddenly, there was a tremendous sizzling noise like a sparkler. At the same time, a bluish-white light filled the room, as if someone had ignited a huge amount of magnesium right before my eyes. I couldn't see a thing. The next instant a powerful blast that felt like hundreds of needles piercing my naked torso threw me violently against the wall.

Within moments my wife, who had been in our barbershop preparing to open for the day, came screaming into the living room, "We've been bombed!" Feeling as if she had just said we were about to die, I grabbed her hand and yanked her outside. The blast was even then knocking the house down around us, and I have no idea how we made it out in time. The next thing I realized, we were across the streetcar avenue crawling in a garden of potatoes.

As headquarters photographer, I had frequently gone to see the destruction wrought by the air raids in nearby Kure, Iwakuni, and Ōtake. Still, I was completely overwhelmed when it happened in Hiroshima. My heart raced wildly with fear. Dust was blasted into the air where it mixed with the ashes of death from the explosion itself to block the sun and then come raining down. It became so utterly dark I couldn't even see my wife's face as she lay right next to me. I squeezed her hand tightly. Her warmth pulsed through me in the darkness, and I felt the joy of being alive.

Ten minutes passed. Fifteen. Beginning at the ground, the darkness lifted around us, and we could see. Afraid that more bombs would follow, we carefully made our way from the garden to the streetcar avenue. We didn't know that an atomic bomb had been dropped. All the houses visible in that dim, smoky light were damaged and tilting over. Roof tiles had fallen. Windows were blown away, and debris filled the street. Ragged and torn electrical lines dangled eerily in the wreckage. It was a scene of pure misery, and I still assumed the bomb had fallen very close by. I realized I had to hurry to my post at the Imperial Headquarters, so I returned to my house to get my things. I found the windows all blown away, and the wall facing the blast was now a gaping hole. Piles of mud plaster filled the living room. There was nothing I could do. I still had to go to work, so I pulled some clothes and my camera from the debris. This was now some thirty to forty minutes after the bombing.

I walked straight along the streetcar avenue from Miyuki Bridge toward Takanobashi. The closer I got to town the more total was the destruction of the buildings. The numbers of burned and otherwise injured people also increased. Where could the bomb have fallen? Puzzled and irritated by this confusion, I finally made it to Takanobashi. It was now about one hour and a half after the bombing.

By this time the fires that had sprung up here and there downtown had spread through the city. The neighborhood across from Takanobashi was already a sea of flames. City Hall and the West Fire Station were blazing uncontrollably. I decided it would be impossible to pass through this conflagration and on into town, so I retreated to the west end of Miyuki Bridge. From there I circled around south of the Hiroshima University campus (then Hiroshima University of Literature and Science) and toward Hiranomachi, but again I was forced to stop. Here too, huge flames roared. Blocked by flaming whirlwinds like bright-red drum cans rolling toward me down a hill, I went back toward the west end of Miyuki Bridge. By now, several hundred people were seeking refuge in that area.

Slightly more than two and a half hours had passed since the bombing and the first round of fires. The people around me seemed barely alive. The majority had grotesquely singed hair as well as gruesome burns on their faces, limbs, and backs – the work of the thermal rays. Their blisters had broken. Their skin hung in shreds. Barefoot children had lost their shoes in melted asphalt.

Those who gathered at Miyuki Bridge were almost all volunteers who had been demolishing houses to make firebreaks. Many were first-or second-year junior high school students; some were housewives who had brought their small children along. In front of the police office near the west end of the bridge, two officers (I couldn't tell from behind whether they were policemen or soldiers) were treating burn victims with cooking oil. With no other medicines available, that cooking oil was all the first aid they could offer. Despite this, they were besieged by crowds of sufferers seeking help. This area in front of

Shortly after 11 a.m. on August 6, 1945; west of Miyuki Bridge (2.3 kilometers from the hypocenter.)

(Photo by Yoshito Matsushige)

this police station had become a temporary relief station.

"I'll get a quick picture of this," I told myself. But as I lifted the camera hanging around my neck, I found it impossible to snap the shutter. The scene before me was so gruesome that I merely stood there, paralyzed by the reality of this hell.

The surroundings were gloomy due to the flames and black smoke, but the eyes of all the victims who had thrown their peeling bodies down on the still-hot August pavement seemed to be focused on me. I saw a tiny baby clinging tightly to the breast of a woman no longer able to move. Another woman was cradling her infant, crying and screaming its name, begging, "Open you eyes! Just open your eyes!" In the midst of all this horror I was unable to take even a single photograph.

But this would not do. I realized I had to break this paralysis and perform my duty, which was to document this horror on film. Despite whatever the sufferers might be thinking, I must take pictures. Then, as though a dam inside me had broken, I raised the camera to my eye and, without taking time to focus, clicked the shutter. After that I relaxed somewhat. Walking slowly five or six meters closer, I raised the camera for a second shot. When I compared my slight injuries to those of so many victims lingering on the border between life and death or passing through their final agony, the scene through my view finder clouded with tears. Those scenes are burned into my retina even to this day. I still feel apologetic to those suffering people, but I was glad I managed to get two photos of that misery. Fulfilling my responsibility gave me a certain calm. To those people lying before me in pain, staring at me and begging for water, I tried to offer consolation and encouragement. "The army relief corps is coming. Just hang on," I told them. Soon I fled from Miyuki Bridge, the sufferers behind me clinging tightly to my heart.

By 2:00 that afternoon, the fires in much of the city had died down. "Looks like I can get downtown. I think I'll go to the newspaper office or the Imperial Headquarters." Thinking, "There'll probably be someone there," I crossed the Miyuki

Bridge again, and headed into town past the campus of Hiroshima University toward Hiranomachi. There was a swimming pool just inside the grounds at the south corner. Riding to work the previous day, August 5, I had passed this pool on my bicycle and noticed that it was filled with water for use against fires. But the tremendous flames that swept through the city had evaporated nearly all the water, and on the white cement bottom lay seven or eight corpses. It was a hideous sight I couldn't bear to examine.

Rubble left by the fires filled and thoroughly blocked the streets. I picked my way gingerly through the smoldering ruins, finally arriving at Nagarekawa, where our newspaper office was located. The scenes that met my eyes on the way were a scorched hell, a city of death. From Fujimichō and Tanakamachi to Nagarekawa, bodies were strewn everywhere. Many were pinned under collapsed buildings where they were evidently burned alive. I was slowly becoming numb to all this. I lost the sense that these bodies before me were actually human corpses.

We reached the office, but no one was there. All that was left of the structure was an empty, smoldering skeleton. East of the old Fukuya building I saw a streetcar blown halfway up onto the sidewalk by the force of the bomb blast. The trees along this wide road were toppled and charred by the blast and the fires. Steel building frames were twisted like taffy. Fallen electrical poles and tangled wires littered the streets. When I saw a scattered collection of military helmets and swords burned reddish-brown, I realized with a jolt that Japan had lost the war.

Walking on to Kamiyachō through white smoke, I noticed the extreme damage done to the buildings: those made of concrete had been transformed into vast, empty shells, while wooden structures were razed completely to the ground. A lonely, burned-out streetcar stood motionless at Hiroshima's largest intersection (the Kamiyachō streetcar stop). From a distance it appeared that people were still inside, so I walked closer to see what had happened. As I stepped up to the entrance, my body went rigid with horror. Ten or more bodies lay piled on top of one another, and I knew then that the intense thermal rays and blast (Kamiyachō was only 200 meters from the hypocenter) had taken their lives instantly. They had been riding along in that streetcar and then were suddenly burned to death. And the horrible expressions on their faces made them look like the terrible *Fudō Myōō (Acala)** that I had seen in pictures.

Then, as now, Kamiyachō was lined with the branch offices of Tokyo-based banks and insurance companies.

At the entrance to each one of those buildings were piled two or three corpses. The famed human shadow imprinted on the steps of the Sumitomo Bank was caused by the intense heat rays. Hardly any survived in this area; it was too close to the hypocenter. I walked through the center of town seeing no one walking, only corpses strewn everywhere. Then, in Fukuromachi and Kokutaijichō, along the streetcar track, I met several people who had come looking for members of their family. They walked around in utter silence, dumbstruck by this cruelly transformed city of death.

In Shirakami Shrine was a huge camphor tree, 300 years old and so big around that three adults could barely encircle it. Its giant branches had almost engulfed the Hiroshima Branch of the Bank of Japan. The tree had been a favorite refuge from the sun's heat, the perfect place to take a break in the shade. The atomic bomb had uprooted and toppled it, but even after its long bout with the flames, the dark, charred trunk retained its shape. Several corpses lay nearby. City Hall was a shell, and the West Fire Station was rubble fallen around the burned-out carcasses of fire engines. They had not even been able to put up a fight against the conflagration.

It was about 5:00 p.m., when I walked back through Takanobashi past the Hiroshima Red Cross Hospital and returned to Miyuki Bridge, still strewn with bodies. At the west end, an Akatsuki Corps* rescue truck approached, and four or five soldiers began carrying the most seriously injured off to a safer place. By this time the peeling, blistered wounds of the burned survivors had already become infested with maggots. The Akatsuki Corps soldiers were taking these wounded to the Ujina National Hospital as well as to their own barracks, but there was a limit to the number they could carry. Many survivors were dragging themselves forward painfully, aimlessly following the lines of people moving toward Ujina.

That evening, about 150 meters southeast of Miyuki Bridge, where the streetcar turns the corner, Chief Suzawa of the Ujina Police Department and several of his officers began issuing victim certificates. The officer who was writing these certificates, Mr. Tokuo Fujita, himself wounded, continued writing until it became too dark. Those who received these certificates presented them to another officer, who, in turn, gave out bags of hardtack. This was how I obtained my sustenance for that night.

For hours as I wandered in that boiling hell, in fact, until I returned home, I had not thought of my wife or home at all. I had completely forgotten about them. On returning home, I saw my wife's healthy face. I hadn't noticed it in the morning when I had left home, but the four-story wood frame fire station directly in front of our house had been utterly destroyed by the blast. The man who had been up in the watchtower at the time had incurred a terrible burn over half his face. Several others had been trapped with the fire trucks under the collapsed building. Also, my wife's niece, Michie Nakamura, a second-year student at Hiroshima Girls' School of Commerce, was horribly injured. She had been helping to demolish buildings with her classmates at the time of the atomic bombing but had managed somehow to escape to our house. Not only were her face, back, and legs covered with burns, the soles of her feet were, too. She had lost both her shoes while escaping from the flames. While I was wandering through the city, my wife had been caring for her niece and the injured man from the fire station. In the dimness of our air-raid shelter, in response to painful cries of, "It hurts! I'm burning!" all she could do was to offer them cool air with a broken paper fan.

It had been a long, bloodcurdling day. As the twilight darkened, the fires that still raged downtown seemed to leap up toward the sky like heat haze. My wife and I found a place to rest our weary bodies in the remains of the fire station, and there we told each other of cry and screams of the *Muken-jigoku* (*Avici Hell*)* we had experienced that day. My wife told me then that, at the time of the explosion, she had seen in one of the mirrors in our barbershop an intense, red fireball. As the curtains of night came down, the flames across the city flared up bright, but then immediately died away, as if somehow touched by the scenes of carnage which their own light revealed. It seemed as though a sacred bonfire was burning for the many, many souls of the dead.

I had walked for two and a half hours downtown through blood-red rubble strewn with corpses, and I never snapped my shutter once. The only pictures I took were the two on the west end of Miyuki Bridge about three hours after the bombing, two more of my house that afternoon before going into town, and one more that evening of the policeman issuing survivor's certificates in Minamimachi – a total of five. I still felt I had done well to get even a few pictures under such extreme circumstances.

I do have a few other photographs of different evils the bomb left in its wake. In March 1945, when the Japanese defeat was approaching, the Cabinet decided the Schoolchildren Evacuation Reinforcement Guidelines. I attended the departure of the first group on April 3, 47 students and 3 teachers from Ōte-machi National School to cover the story. This group went off to live in a temple, though some eventually ran back home. From all of Hiroshima approximately 9,000 children were evacuated. These children returned to Hiroshima after the war was over. When they met their parents after over three months of painful separation, they seemed to burst with joy, running over to them and holding them tightly. But too many of those children had to just stand by, watching the reunions tearfully. They were waiting for parents who had been killed by the bomb, parents they would never see again.

I wonder how their teachers explained this to them. "All of you whose parents haven't come, gather over here," they said. As I filmed those extremes of joy and sadness, the heat of pure rage welled up in my heart. If not for the war, these children's parents would be alive, this tragedy would not have occurred. I took those photographs in sorrow and resentment, in full appreciation that war is a heinous evil. This event and the pictures of hell I photographed at Miyuki Bridge on the day of the sixth are permanently etched in my mind.

"Since wars begin in the minds of men, it is in the minds of men that the defenses of peace must be constructed." We must never forget this statement from the UNESCO Charter, and we must never again repeat the tragedy of war nor the use of a nuclear weapon. The cruel scars of the atomic bombing remain with us even now, in the loss of the hundreds of thousands who died on that day, in the pain of those who have continued to suffer and die ever since. I was there and I lived, and I have devoted the rest of my life to praying for the souls of the victims and conveying the horrors of the atomic bomb to the next generation.

I Cared for My Pupils, Putting Up Mosquito Netting in the Schoolyard

by Hiroshi Sasamura

By March of 1945 the war at home was becoming more intense. From the windows of our elementary school building in Hiroshima I could see groups of black fighter planes flying off toward Kure, just like flocks of birds. I felt the day of the decisive battle on our homeland drawing closer. I suspected that I would soon be drafted and sent off to war.

For protection from firebombs*, we were ordered to remove the ceiling boards above the corridor in the schoolhouse. Though I hated to destroy that grand old building, two or three male teachers and myself tore the boards off one by one. While we were at this task, one of the teachers received a telephone call informing him that he had received a draft paper* and should return home immediately. He left us looking grim, not even bothering to wash his dirty face. The next day another teacher received a draft paper and returned to his hometown as well. Thus, the violent winds of war were now sweeping through the schools.

In early April we began to prepare for mass evacuations of the children to the countryside. Pupils from the third to sixth grades were divided up according to their neighborhoods, with one teacher for every twenty pupils. These groups then formed four larger groups that departed from the school on April 15 and 17, each heading for one of four temples. During those two days we held a final ceremony for the departing pupils. A representative of the pupils gave a little speech in front of his schoolmates. Then the first and second graders lined up along the road in

Mealtime at a Children's Evacuation Site (Shōbōji Temple, Mirasaka-chō, Futami-gun, Hiroshima Prefecture)(1945)
(Photo courtesy of Yōzō Umeno)

front of the school entrance to wave to the older children as they took leave of school and family, heading for temples and schools in the unfamiliar countryside.

Life at the temples was extremely difficult. Food was in short supply – not even the children could eat their fill. Moreover, all soon became flea*-infested, and the girls' hair filled with lice*. After about a month of this life, one child, unable to endure the pain of separation from his parents, stole off at night and began walking toward Hiroshima. When his absence was discovered a great furor arose at the temple, and they immediately telephoned the school. After several hours' search we finally found the child. I told him, "If you want to see your parents that badly, you may stay with them one night. But the next day you must return to the temple because Hiroshima will definitely be bombed soon." The following day I delivered him back to the

82

temple.

Summer came, but we had no holiday from school. The first and second-graders continued to come to school, as did third graders and up who could not be evacuated. These latter were those who had to see their doctor frequently, bed-wetters, and any other children ill-suited for community life.

August 6th arrived. The presence of enemy planes in the sky the preceding night had triggered a state of alert, but the yellow air-raid warning was lifted at around 7:30 a.m., letting us know the planes were gone. Parents had been told to keep their children at home during such a warning, but to send them to school as usual when it was lifted.

Because the principal was busy with some other obligation, I, as head teacher, assembled the other teachers for the morning meeting to discuss the day's activities. At 8:05, as time was running out, I put off the remaining items on the agenda for later and closed the meeting. I then rang the bell hanging under the eaves outside the window to announce the children's morning assembly. We teachers walked out of the staff room together and headed for the playground, rounding up along the way any children we found in the building and schoolyard. At the time, in order to increase food supplies, the central part of the playground had been turned into a sweet potato garden. Tending this garden was one of the children's duties. The only open area remaining for assembly, therefore, was the space between the sweet potato garden and the school house. One hundred twenty first and second graders and more than twenty children from the upper grades gathered at this spot, and I stepped up to the platform to begin telling a story.

The sky was cloudless and clear. The sun beat down, and the day promised to be hot. I felt sorry for the pupils standing under the blazing sun and impulsively announced, "Boys go stand under the willow to the right; girls, under the willow to the left." The children happily complied, and I began the story. In the middle of the story, I noticed two or three sixth-grade boys standing in the back under the willow tree's shade staring up at the sky. In retrospect, I think these boys had either seen the A-bomb plane itself or heard the droning roar. Because the warning had been lifted, I had no reason to think planes were flying over Hiroshima. I was not paying attention to the sky; I was loudly telling my story. I was about to admonish them, as usual, to pay attention, but was abruptly cut short: "Be sure you –"

Suddenly a white light shot across the clear sky like a powerful ribbon-flash of magnesium. I may have heard a whooshing sound. "We've been bombed!" I thought instinctively, and shouted "Take shelter!"

This order meant that everyone should immediately let go of anything in their hands and crouch low on the ground. This was because standing maximized the possibility of injury from the blast. We knew we might be bombed one day, and had all been trained to adopt this posture automatically. The children standing in the shade probably dropped into this position but I never knew, as I had to drop from the platform onto the ground immediately. Just when I stepped back to climb backwards down the steps, the two-story wooden schoolhouse exploded, raining a shower of debris atop the children and myself.

I have no idea how much time passed. When I regained consciousness I found I had been thrown three or four meters from the platform, and rubble from the school building piled over my body. I heard other objects continuing to fall from above. The sky, so clear earlier, was completely black. The air was so clogged with dust that I could hardly see. I was lying on my stomach. "I'm not dead, I'm alive," was my first thought. Probably no one knows the joy of life so well as he who has stood on the threshold of death. Then I noticed a girl lying under my left armpit. I wondered if a sixth grader and I had been thrown together, but a closer look revealed that she was one of the teachers. I asked her, "If you can move, crawl out, find out what has happened to the children, and report back to me." Though it was not reasonable to expect that my two arms were strong enough to move the schoolhouse collapsed atop me, I nevertheless tried to prop myself up. After a while the woman teacher, whose name was Kitamura, managed to extricate herself. But she did not return and I learned nothing of the situation outside the rubble.

As I lay face down I gradually felt something lukewarm dripping from my scalp to my forehead. Realizing I had incurred a head wound I became afraid that I would lose consciousness. "I must free myself while I still have my senses!" I thought. (Later on I seemed to remember a long nail sticking into my back at this point, but I don't know how or when I got it out and I don't remember any pain.) I was then able to work my way through the debris and crawl out to the playground.

All was dark as dusk, and I saw that most of the children had somehow congregated at the sweet potato garden, where they were standing and crying. Being under the willow at the time of the blast had given them some protection from the falling building, and most were not badly injured. They were huddled together, crying, "Mother! Mother! Teacher!" Just a short time ago they had been lined up next to their closest friends. Now they could not even recognize each other in the darkness and through the white dust covering their faces and hair. Walking over, I addressed the group loudly, "This is your teacher. I am with you so don't be afraid. Now stop crying and sit down! And don't move until I tell you to!" My voice, neither clearly angry nor clearly authoritative, nevertheless got the children to sit. I encircled the group with the rope that had been stretched around the sweet potato garden, then ran off for help.

Realizing I must first go to the office of the Civilian Guard*, I passed through the school gate and ran out into the neighborhood. I thought the school had suffered a direct attack, and wanted help freeing the others from the debris right away. I ran 50 meters, then 100 – no matter how far I went it was still dark. Running down the streetcar avenue I noticed all the houses tilting this way and that. I saw no one, but maybe this was because my mind was so frenzied and agitated. I remember seeing only an old horse, lying dead on its side.

When I finally reached the office, only one member was in sight. He lay completely still on the road, and I assumed he had been thrown by the force of the blast from the observation deck on the roof. No help was available here, so I turned to hurry back to the school. Just at that moment I saw a fire starting northeast of me, a large red flame climbing up through the dusk. Then it died down, and something like white smoke rose up in its place. The next instant, that white smoke burst into an even larger flame. That fire was terrifying. I was sixteen years old at the time of the Great Kantō Earthquake of 1923, and I remembered my teacher telling me that more people died in the ensuing fires than from the earthquake itself. Fearing that Hiroshima would go up in flames, I hastened back to the school.

Upon returning I found the pupils waiting exactly as I had left them, their expressions still dazed. I remember telling them, "All right, everyone stand up. Fires are heading this way, so we're moving over there." I led them to the southwest corner of the playground, the farthest spot from the school building. Then I told them, "If your parents come, you can leave with them." Next, I set about trying to free the people trapped under the building. I found one teacher who had been struck on the back and was unable to move; another was lying injured on the ground. Along with those teachers who still retained their strength, I searched through the debris and helped free the trapped children. I considered it my responsibility to see that not one child died or suffered injury, so it was with deep sadness that I discovered two of the little girls I picked up from the debris had already died. They both had tiny name badges sewn by their mothers onto the fronts of their blouses. I called out their names repeatedly as I held them in my arms and shook them, but no answer came. One child had lost both ears, and her white summer shirt was soaked red with blood. I felt so sorry. I spread a straw mat under the shade of a tree, and gently laid her on it.

When all the children seemed to have been extricated from the building, I allowed myself a short rest. I had absolutely no sense of time at this point. I was wearing a bandage around my head like a headband. When I returned from the Civilian Guard wiping the blood from my forehead with my arm, a woman teacher noticed my bleeding and wrapped a cloth around my head. But when I had some time to take stock, I saw that the wound was on the top of my head, completely outside the wrapped area. In addition, I had been wearing canvas shoes that morning as I stood on the platform. Now I saw that one of them was gone. I had been running around barefoot and had not even realized it. Later on, this made me realize how intensely absorbed we had been in our duties.

Meanwhile, the fires were gradually spreading, and hot, black smoke poured onto the playground. Along with the smoke appeared crowds of people, injured and wounded from the blast, seeking refuge at the playground. The preset emergency plan called for doctors and the neighborhood chief to gather at the school to provide relief. As nearly everything was destroyed, there was no true relief we could offer. The best we could do was to have the injured lie down in a corner of the playground and give them water.

The children were taken to the southwest corner of the field farthest from the schoolhouse. There we believed they would be safe from fire; a woodpile gathered from dismantled buildings was also in this area. It had been carried up to the school for firewood in preparing school lunches. Suddenly that pile of wood caught fire. I ran to get water from the fire-prevention water cistern and extinguish the fire before it got out of hand. I was utterly mystified that this wood, nowhere near any of the fires, could have spontaneously ignited like that.

One after another, parents and other family members appeared to collect their children. In the end I was left with about ten who had no place to go because their parents were dead and their houses burned down. We decided to lay a straw mat in a corner of the schoolyard. We had the children sit down, draped some mosquito netting* over them, and took care of them all night. One of the girls had a badly swollen head wound, round like a pomegranate. In a weak voice she said, "Teacher, I have to go to the bathroom." The thought that she would have to die tonight without seeing her parents made my chest hurt. "Go where you are, and I'll get you all cleaned up later," I told her.

Darkness fell, and the night of the day of the atomic bombing was upon us. The remaining pupils and two teachers spent the next few days huddled in one corner of the playground.

Forty-one years have passed. This year too, August sixth came and went. A woman who saw my article and picture in the A-bomb commemoration issue of the Hiroshima Naka-ku Ward Newsletter happened to meet me one day in town. "It's you, that teacher!" she said, grasping my hand. "I was a sixth grader then. Because you happened to put us under the trees that day, we escaped without serious injury. I saw the airplane that day, you know." She spoke with deep emotion of that day in the past. She went on to tell me that she had not told her children of her experience. Those words resounded in my heart. The town of Hiroshima has been greatly altered to conform to the image of a "City of Peace." The boulevards are grand, and the trees have grown stately and beautiful. Yet it grieves me to think that there are still people scattered throughout the city who live in secret fear of what the atomic bomb may have done to their bodies, who tell no one of their experience for fear it will hurt their daughters' chances for marriage.

What Does It Mean to Live in Hiroshima?

by Akihiro Takahashi

One of our most powerful talents as human beings, they say, is our ability to forget. But I have never forgotten for a moment the horror of that day. No matter how painful the memory, I have told myself, I must never forget. And when my thoughts turn to this subject, I am forced to realize that August sixth marked the real starting point of my life. Almost as if it were yesterday, one scene after another of that grotesque calamity continues to stream through my mind.

At 8:15 a.m., on August 6, 1945, the world's first atomic bomb exploded in the air above Hiroshima. The devilish flash, combined with a deafening roar and shock waves powerful enough to shake the Earth on its axis, soon reduced the city to ruins, burning away every living thing in its path.

I was fourteen years old, a second-year student at a Hiroshima municipal junior high school. In the schoolyard at the time of the bombing, moving into formation for the morning assembly, I was about 1.4 kilometers from the hypocenter. There was a total of about 150 students, including about 60 members of one second year class. Both the yellow air-raid and red air-raid warnings had just been canceled, but somehow a B-29 was approaching in the sky above us. "Look! A B-29!" we shouted, pointing up and following the plane with our eyes.

"Attention!" ordered the class president, and we all stopped what we were doing and faced the front. Just then, a tremendous roar filled the air and everything turned pitch black.

Five or ten minutes later, the smoke finally cleared away, and the schoolyard came into view. I had been blown some ten meters back by the blast; my classmates had also been blown forward, backward, left and right, lying scattered all around me. The school building had completely collapsed and none of the neighboring houses still stood. Except for one or two here and there, the buildings all around us and off into the distance had also disappeared. For a bewildered second I thought, "Hiroshima has vanished!"

Coming to my senses, I quickly examined myself. My uniform was burned and tattered. The skin on the back of my head, my back, my arms and legs had peeled like rags, red flesh was painfully exposed to the air. Glass fragments protruded from my skin in several places. We had been drilled every day to run, in the event of an air raid, as quickly as possible to the river. Remembering our routine evacuation drills now, I hurriedly left the schoolyard and, reaching the street, made my way alone toward the river. On the way I heard someone calling my name, "Takahashi, Takahashi!" Turning around, I saw my classmate Tatsuya Yamamoto. We used to walk to school together every day. He was burned and injured as badly as I. He cried out loudly, "Mama, Mama...!" Then he asked me, "What's happened to my house in Kusatsu? If my parents are dead, can I live with you?" He talked on and on, sort of mumbling away. Sometimes I'd try to encourage him, other times I angrily scolded, "It won't do any good to cry. We just have to get to the river!" So saying, I pulled him along as we fled.

I saw a line of A-bomb survivors looking dazed, dragging their legs and coming toward me. Their arms dangled oddly in front of them, and their clothes were in tatters. Many were virtually naked. It was exactly like a procession of ghosts. I saw one man with hundreds of glass shards piercing his body from the waist up. The skin of another man had peeled off his entire upper body, exposing a mass of red flesh. A woman was covered in blood, one eyeball grotesquely dangling out of its socket. Next to a mother whose skin had completely peeled off lay a loudly crying baby, its body an unprotected mass of red flesh. A number of corpses lay scattered about. A dead woman's internal organs had burst out onto the ground around her. It was utterly gruesome, a living hell indescribable in words. We ran to the river as fast as we could. All the streets and paths leading to the riverbank were blocked by the wreckage of toppled houses. It seemed impossible to get through. We crawled desperately over and through the ruins until we finally managed to find the river. Luckily, just when we emerged from the debris, we came upon a small wooden bridge that had somehow managed to survive the blast. At the moment we were stepping out onto the bridge, tongues of fire suddenly licked out from the collapsed houses on both sides of the street. In a matter of seconds, the whole area

Drawing by an A-bomb Survivor:
Escaping with my friend across a small wooden bridge over the
Yamate River. (This bridge no longer exists; the Yamate River is now
the Ōta River Flood Channel.) (by Akihiro Takahashi)

91

was a sea of flame. Crackling loud as thunder, the pillar of fire shot up to heights of four, five meters and more. Fortunately, we were already beyond this danger, but if we had been one step slower in making our escape, we would undoubtedly have been enveloped in those flames and burned to death.

I walked across the bridge. I didn't notice when it happened, but Yamamoto was gone. I couldn't find him. Once on the other side, when I allowed myself to relax a little, my back started stinging, and then I felt a tremendous rush of heat and pain. I still remember immersing myself in the river about three times, where the coolness of the water was as priceless medicine to my burning body. "Ah, I'm safe," I thought, and instantly my body shook with long-repressed sobs. After climbing up from the river, someone directed me to a temporary rescue center in a bamboo forest atop a hill. There I received emergency aid and rested for a while. Then rain began to fall – black rain, like no rain I had ever seen. Huge drops plopped noisily on the ground. I watched anxiously. Was there really such a thing as black rain?

I waited for it to let up, then started walking home. After a while, again I heard someone calling my name. I turned and saw Tokujirō Hatta crouching on the ground. He was another friend who used to walk to school with Yamamoto and me. "Takahashi, help me! Take me home with you!" he begged, groaning. For some reason, the bottoms of his feet were burned so badly that the skin had peeled, revealing the red flesh beneath; but somehow the rest of his body had escaped any serious burns or cuts. He obviously could not walk. He said someone had brought him this far on the back of a bicycle. Though I myself was seriously burned, I could not abandon a friend seeking help and continue on my way alone. I decided immediately to somehow take Hatta along with me. But how? Except for the soles of his feet, his burns and lacerations were relatively mild. Thinking the matter through, I decided that there were two ways to get him home without having his feet touch the ground:

one was to have him crawl on his hands and knees; the other was to lean him back on his heels while I supported him. Thus we began our trek, alternating between these two methods. Plodding along slower than cows, step after agonizing step, somehow we managed to help each other along.

At one point, sitting exhausted on the roadside, I happened to look behind me. I couldn't believe it. My great-uncle and my great-aunt (my grandfather's younger brother and his wife) were walking toward us! I shouted at the top of my lungs to try to get my great uncle and aunt to stop. My great-uncle was a bit deaf so he couldn't hear my shouts. He strode purposefully right on by. When my aunt came along I yelled loudly to her and she stopped. She just stood there at first, shocked to see us; then she ran ahead quickly and brought my uncle back. They were returning home to Kusatsu from a relative's Buddhist memorial service in the countryside. We have a saying in Japan, "Like meeting the Buddha in Hell," and that was exactly how we felt about meeting my great-aunt and great-uncle. They even happened to have with them two large rice balls in case of an emergency. I gobbled mine down quickly, and even now I can vividly recall the taste. Since we hardly ever had white rice in those days, it was exceedingly delicious. They offered the other rice ball to Hatta, but he weakly refused it.

Once rescued and returned safely to our homes, I realized that we two severely burned boys – no matter how much we helped each other – could never have managed the more than six kilometers to my house from school.

I was unconscious for about three weeks once I got home. I was able to receive treatment for my burns, however. Twice a day, morning and night, an otolaryngologist came to my home. Ordinarily, otolaryngologists do not treat burns, but considering the nearly total lack of physicians and nurses in the city at that time, I believe I was extremely fortunate to find any medical practitioner at all to help me. Actually, it was my grandfather who encountered Dr. Hayashi by chance near our house and begged him to come and see me. We had known him for some time; I and my brothers had regularly gone to him for checkups. With his help, I hovered on the border of life and death for a year and a half. I survived, but "I died nine deaths to live." Two days after the bombing, however, my friend Tokujirō Hatta fell ill with acute radiation sickness and died. My other friend, Tatsuya Yamamoto, passed away a month and a half later of the same illness.

I have lived, but my right elbow and all the fingers except the thumb on my right hand are bent out of shape. I have keloid burns on both arms and legs, and a 'black nail' continues to grow on my right index finger. (You may have seen two samples of this 'black nail' that fell off and are on display at the Hiroshima Peace Memorial Museum.) I am also afflicted with chronic hepatitis, believed to be an aftereffect of radiation (certified as such by the government). I have been hospitalized fourteen times since 1971 and am still undergoing treatment. I suffer from many other ailments as well, so much so that the only wards in the hospital I haven't been in are pediatrics, maternity and psychiatric wards.

I fear for my life every day and, at times, my frail health has brought me close to despair. I have often wondered, "Why should I go on suffering like this?" But each time I remember that I survived. In this way I have lived until today.

Of my sixty or so classmates, approximately fifty were killed by the atomic bomb. To date, I have confirmed that fourteen – including myself – are still living. Thus, I am one of the very few who survived. "We cannot let our friends' deaths be in vain. Our destiny and responsibility as survivors lies in handing down to future generations the soundless voices of the victims we knew." I have lived to this day with this conviction etched in my heart, urging myself to live by it. Before reaching adulthood, before getting to do anything with their lives, my friends succumbed to the atomic bombing and died in agony. How bitter they must have felt! Thinking of them fills me with a recognition of the preciousness of life. Hiroshima, I believe, is the place where we should reconfirm of the meaning of life and ceaselessly ask what it is to be alive, and learn to revere life accordingly. "I have actually survived until today!" – This is my honest feeling.

Hiroshima is not merely an historical fact; it is a continuous warning and lesson for the future. War is caused by human beings, and it leads not only to one's own death but to the deaths of loved ones, parents, brothers and sisters, teachers, and friends. A nuclear war, in particular, has neither winners nor losers. It holds in store nothing less than the extinction of the human species, the effective destruction of the planet itself. If human beings don't eliminate nuclear weapons, then the weapons will surely eliminate us. Nuclear war, I believe, is truly a challenge to human reason and ideals. Human beings should abolish nuclear weapons and thus create world peace. Now we should transcend all pain, sadness and hatred from the past, join hands with each other regardless of differences of race or national boundaries, and change the flow of history from distrust to trust, from hostility to reconciliation, and from division to harmony.

One person's strength is limited, of course, but no one is completely powerless. Unless someone starts something, we will have nothing. I firmly believe that peace can come about only through the cumulative efforts of individual citizens everywhere. Peace will not simply be handed to us as a gift; it will not come walking up to greet us; and, finally, it will not arrive if we simply sit and wait. Peace is something we must create, something we must actively talk about, act on, build upon, and then strive to make happen.

World peace will not arrive at a stroke. We have to build peace from where we are, beginning right around us. In other words, we must begin in our homes, in our schools, in our workplaces, in our communities. Then, standing on that foundation, we can bring peace to Japan and the world.

Without losing our focus on the problems of war and nuclear weapons, we need to broaden our perspective. Many other factors threaten peace, including global warming, the population explosion, starvation, growing numbers of refugees, violence, and human rights abuses. In fact, we need to look at the factors threatening peace right here in Japan. Nuclear power accidents, AIDS, bullying, corruption among politicians and high-level bureaucrats, scandals at banks and securities companies, financial bankruptcies and depression—these phenomena have the potential to unleash forces that will destroy whatever happiness we have achieved. These are the "negative assets" of the 20th century, and the ones who will inherit them are our own children, grandchildren, and future generations. If our children fail to respond properly to the terrible problems we bequeath them, the 21st century could very well be the last for human life on Earth.

I hope the younger generations will make Hiroshima their starting point and view the world from a more global perspective. To that end, and to make the 21st century a century of light and hope, I intend to continue to devote whatever energy I have left to telling my A-bomb experience and spreading the spirit of Hiroshima.

What I Want to Say Now

by Akiko Takakura

Three colors express for me the day the atomic bomb fell on Hiroshima: black, red, and brown. It was black when the explosion cut off sunlight and plunged the world into darkness. Red was the color of blood pouring out of all the broken and cut people. Red was also the color of the flames that burned everything in the city. Brown was the color of the burnt, peeling skin exposed to heat rays said to be between 3,000 and 4,000 degrees Celsius.

I was 19 years old, an employee of the Hiroshima Bank, located at No.17 Kamiya-chō. That day dawned crystal clear, and the midsummer sun was soon beating down on the earth. After a yellow air-raid warning, the all-clear sounded at 7:31. I arrived at work at 8:10. I was cleaning the desks with my friend as usual when a white light flashed outside. I lost consciousness, so I don't know what happened after that. I do know that I was blown to the floor by the blast. I have no idea how much time passed before the sound of my friend crying "Mother! Mother!" brought me back to consciousness. Astonished, I thought, "We were hit. The bank was bombed." I could see nothing in the pitch black. The bank staff had often instructed us, "If there's an air attack, get to the military drill ground* right away." The drill ground was about 200 meters from the bank. Realizing that we needed to escape immediately, I called to my friend in the darkness, "Let's get out of here!" Though she had been working right next to me, her pained voice now came from some distance away. "I can't get up. Go ahead and go." When the blast had blown her to the floor, it had broken something in her spine. At that time I thought she was just feeling sick, so in the scant light that was returning I searched around my feet. I caught water spouting from a broken water pipe in a fragment of an iron helmet. I carried it to her and poured it on her head. After I had done this five or six times, I was surprised when she was able to get up. We held hands tightly and said, "Let's run together." Then we left the building. Outside we found a sea of flames, even behind the bank. The fires sprang up quickly here because Hiroshima Bank was only 260 meters from the hypocenter. "What shall we do?" Thinking together to save our lives, we decided to go to the Sumitomo Bank next door because it had a high firewall. In desperation, we climbed the wall and jumped down on the other side in the Sumitomo Bank.

We were amazed by what we found in that bank. Smashed desks and chairs were tossed in heaps. Employees lay covered in blood where they had evidently been killed instantly. We could only gasp. Soon flames began to spread inside the building as well. We went out to the main streetcar street and crouched in front of a fire cistern. The whole city was engulfed in flames. I cannot express the fear and disorientation we felt as we tried to decide what to do, assailed by the intense heat and smoke. Every two or three minutes a whirling fireball would hurtle toward us. "Ooh! Help!" Five or six of us injured but still alive cried out in grief, anger, and fear when burning winds blew toward us. No scene of my life is more painful to remember. Later, huge black raindrops began to fall. Struggling to breathe among the hot flames, we craned our necks and opened our mouths, moving our heads back and forth to catch the black drops and soothe our parched throats. When the fire died down a bit, we walked toward the drill ground.

The streets were piled with the reddish-brown corpses of those who were killed instantly as they walked along. It was painful to walk by them. I tried to walk steadily, but my legs trembled, maybe because of shock. Our progress was slowed by continual-

Drawing by an A-bomb Survivor:
Left Hand with Fingertips Melted by the Atomic Bomb.

(by Akiko Takakura)

ly stopping to avoid stepping on bodies. I saw one corpse with burning fingers. Her hand was raised and her fingers were on fire, blue flames burning them down to stumps. A light charcoal-colored liquid was oozing onto the ground. When I think of those hands cradling beloved children and turning the pages of books, even now my heart fills with a deep sadness.

At the drill ground, the burnt field was strewn with what must have been dead soldiers. Overwhelmed by the calamity I had been suffering since morning, I was utterly stunned, unable to think. I lay down on the field, now nothing but dirt. Again, I don't know how much time passed, but at dusk I suddenly vomited what must have been the remnants of my breakfast–corn, soybean draff, and imported rice. I vomited bloody phlegm twice. I knew then that I, too, would die in that place. I felt chagrined that, despite the countless corpses all around, it never occurred to me that I, a human being like them, might also face death. I had been taught from an early age that after we die we meet our loved ones again in another world. I began to feel that I would soon go someplace far from my parents and siblings.

When night came, paper still left in buildings caught fire and burned red, fluttering down as sparks in the dark sky. Though it was the hottest time of the summer, we shivered with cold at midnight. My friend complained, "I'm freezing." I searched the area and found a burnt tin sheet and laid it on top of her. Her shaking gradually quieted. I found another tin sheet for myself and lay under it.

When dawn came, I heard shoe-clad feet walking from the west across the soundless drill ground. I told my friend, "People wearing shoes are coming." The footsteps stopped near us, and we heard a voice say, "You girls survived. Good for you. Cheer up, a relief squad is on the way." The man, a middle-aged military doctor, started walking toward where the Eleventh Infantry Regiment had been. He was the first person we had seen fully dressed and wearing shoes since the bombing.

During the night of the 6th, I thought, "I'm going to die here soon," but the kind, encouraging words of the doctor gave me the will to live. "I'm going to live, I've got to live." I cannot express how grateful I was to hear his words

I learned later that I had sustained 102 lacerations on my back, two serious bruises, and two burns.

To Children Who Don't Know the Atomic Bomb
by Akiko Takakura

8:15 a.m. on August 6, 1945,
a very clear morning.

The mother preparing her baby's milk,
the old man watering his potted plants,
the old woman offering flowers at her Buddhist altar,
the young boy eating breakfast,
the father starting work at his company,
the thousands walking to work on the street,
all died.
Not knowing an atomic bomb would be dropped,
they lived as usual.
Suddenly, a flash.
"Ah!"
Just as they saw it,
people in houses were shoved over and smashed.
People walking on streets were blown away.
People were burned—faces, arms, legs—all over.
People were killed, all over
the city of Hiroshima
by a single bomb.

Those who died.
A hundred? No. A thousand? No. Ten thousand?
No, many, many more than that.
More people than we can count
died, speechless,
knowing nothing.
Others suffered terrible burns,
horrific injuries.
Some were thrown so hard
their stomachs ripped open,
their spines broke.
Whole bodies filled with glass shards.
Clothes disappeared,
burned and tattered.

Fires came right after the explosion.

Hiroshima engulfed in flames.
Everyone fleeing, not knowing where
they were or where to go.
Everyone barefoot,
crying tears of anger and grief,
hair sticking up, looking like *Ashura**,
they ran on broken glass, smashed roofs
along a long, wide road of fire.
Blood flowed.
Burned skin peeled and dangled.
Whirlwinds of fire raged here and there.
Hundreds, thousands of fire balls
30-centimeters across
whirled right at us.
It was hard to breathe in the flames,
hard to see in the smoke.

What will become of us?
Those who survived, injured and burned,
shouted, "Help! Help!" at the top of their lungs.
One woman walking on the road
died and then
her fingers burned,
a blue flame shortening them like candles,
a gray liquid trickling down her palms
and dripping to the ground.
Whose fingers were those?
More than 50 years later,
I remember that blue flame,
and my heart nearly bursts
with sorrow.

Endlessly Calling for Mother

by Chisako Takeoka

August 6, 4 a.m. The dawn stars were still shining. I was a member of the Women's Volunteer Labor Corps* helping to manufacture manned (*kamikaze*) torpedos in a secret military factory. I returned home just before dawn after working all night.

I aired my *futon* and did some cleaning for the first time in a long time. I had promised to go with a couple friends to Miyajima, so as I was leaving I took a small mirror out of my pocket and looked at my face. Just then, flash!! A tremendous booming sound followed immediately. I have no idea how many seconds or minutes went by before I came to, but I found I had flown over my house and landed in the field on the other side. What could have happened? I looked at the sky. A giant soot-colored cloud was boiling up and spreading out.

My house was tilting over. The roof tiles and glass were blown away. I thought, "Oh no, they dropped a firebomb." I wanted to run and hide in the house, but blood was gushing from my head and I found I couldn't get up. After some time, I managed to get to my hands and knees and crawl to my house. I looked in. I still couldn't see any evidence of a firebomb. Thinking, "This is strange," I went outside again. My neighbors were coming out of their houses with terrible injuries to their heads and faces. Looking up the street in front of our house, I saw crowds of burned people streaming our way calling, "Mother! Water, water, give me water. I'm hot. Help!" The skin was peeling from their shoulders. The hair on their heads stood straight up. They were so dirty and damaged I couldn't even tell men from women.

Small children separated from their parents were screaming. When I thought they had just fallen down, I looked again and they were no longer breathing. Children calling for their mothers. Mothers calling for their children. One after the next they toppled and died. I shared the food I had and put ointment on burns.

My house, the floors covered with fragments of broken glass, was full of people breathing with in gasps. Without food, without medicine, I climbed alone along the mountain behind our house and came to the entrance of an air-raid shelter. It was full of injured people. I looked from the mountain at downtown Hiroshima and saw a sea of fire. My home was in Koi Uemachi, the westernmost part of the city, about 3 kilometers from the hypocenter. I wondered what was happening to my mother. I knew she was somewhere in those flames. Was she dead or alive? I shouted, "Mother! Stay alive! You can't die!"

My mother was a nurse at Hiroshima Second Army Hospital. One of the men from my neighborhood put a blanket on me and said, "Chī-chan, all you can do now is wait. You can go look for your mother in the morning."

Morning, August 7. When the eastern sky started to lighten, I went home. I found stains from the black rain on the *futon* I had been airing. I wet my air-raid hood with water and put it on my head. I put water in my water bottle, and left. I walked to Koi Bridge. Because Koi was three kilometers from the hypocenter, we were spared the fire, but most houses were pushed over and uninhabitable. Crossing Koi Bridge, I walked still further. When I crossed Tenma Bridge, I saw the factory I had worked in. It was nothing but a still-flaming steel skeleton. I kept going, and as I approached the hypocenter, the flames and smoke grew stronger. I saw no one walking around. All alone I searched in the flames and smoke for my mother. I reached Aioi Bridge. Everything was burned. The round dome of the

Hiroshima Prefectural Industrial Promotion Hall (now the A-bomb Dome) was standing like the dead skeleton of the grand building it had been.

I glanced down into the river. It was so full of bodies I could hardly see the water. I kept thinking, "I can't believe my eyes. It's terrible. What could have done all this?"

The bodies of the people floating in the river were swollen to twice or three times their normal size. Overhead I heard the whine of a B29, but I lacked the energy to take cover.

"Mother! Where are you? Please be alive!" Tears flowing, I kept calling her in a voice choked by smoke and sobbing. Looking up the river, I saw three men struggling to lift bodies out of the river and onto the bank. I crossed Aioi Bridge with great difficulty and approached them. "Did you come looking for

Drawing by an A-bomb Survivor:
Loading the Dead onto Trucks (near Aioi Bridge)   (by Miharu Hōki)

someone?" one of the men called when he saw me. "When they're all swollen up like this, you can't tell who is who. You better look for something they were wearing or carrying," he suggested. My mother had three gold teeth in the front of her mouth. I picked up two sticks and went around opening up the mouths of about 40 people to see their front teeth. Their lips were swollen to three or four centimeters.

The men happened to be members of the medical corps from the army hospital where my mother worked, but they said, "Everyone at the hospital had blood flowing from their mouths, noses, and ears. Almost all of them are dead. We were saved by a miracle."

Thinking, "My mother's dead. She could be floating somewhere in this river," I trudged back over the Aioi Bridge and returned to Takajō-machi. My aunt and a ten-year old cousin lived near there, so I tried to figure out where they should be. Finally I found the little stones that marked the entrance to their house. I began to dig around where the kitchen should have been. "No!" The two were sitting there facing each other. Lying on their hipbones were intact skulls, now just clean white bones. I took out my handkerchief, wrapped up some of their bones, and walked back to Sakan-chō. Again, I heard the eerie sound of a B29. This time, I hid near a water cistern. I saw a young mother tightly grasping her young baby. Both were dead. The lower half of the mother's body was charred. When I saw that mother and child, I was filled with grief and rage. I cried and cried.

August 8. I went out again that morning searching for my mother but couldn't find her. That evening, thought I was exhausted, we burned several hundred nameless, pitiful people in the playground at Koi National School.

August 9. Despite air-raid sirens, I searched again, hoping my mother was still alive. My mother's brothers arrived at our house covered with burns and other injuries. I had nothing to give them to eat and no medicine. The smell of sweat and pus from their burns was horrible. Maggots were crawling around in their wounds.

August 10. I searched for my mother in the direction of Kan'on Bridge. The center of the bridge was nearly broken. Looking down from the top of that twisted bridge, I saw a floating corpse wrapped in a *futon*. I knew at a glance it wasn't my mother because of the long hair drifting in the water.

August 11. This time, an old man from my neighborhood went with me. We searched the classrooms at Eba National School several times but couldn't find her. The man started calling her name in a loud voice. Someone lying near us lifted her head slightly and called my name. "Oh, mother. You're my mother, right?" I hugged her tight. She was covered with bandages over her whole head and face. Her right side was burned black. The man who was with me got out two tomatoes and fed them to her. She had lain there for six days with nothing but water.

August 12. I came back to the school with a large handcart to get my mother and bring her home. I took off the bandages and was shocked. "Oh no! You have no right eye!" No iris, no pupil, no white. It was covered with red flesh. The bone of her nose was broken and exposed from bridge to base. The bomb's flash entered her right eye and blew it right out. Glass fragments were still piercing her face in several places, but we had no way to take proper care of her. I heard that the Pharmaceutical Department of the army hospital had been evacuated to the national school in Hesaka. I put my mother on a bicycle-drawn cart and took her there. I was told, "The army doctors all died. The nurses, too. They just vomited blood and died one after the next. All we have left is one veterinarian."

He looked at my mother's eye and said, "If we don't operate immediately she'll lose her left eye too." We put a straw mat down on the floor of the classroom and lay my mother on it. The four orderlies braced to hold her body still. The veterinarian began the operation. There was no anesthetic or any sort of painkiller. Gripping a scalpel in his right hand, he cut out my mother's right eye. She was fully alert. She groaned in a voice that sounded like death throes. I was sitting in the hall outside the classroom. I heard my mother's voice and the sound of thrashing. I was beside myself with fear and thought my heart would burst. At 17, I again felt I was in a living hell. Purple spots had appeared all over my body. My hair was falling out. I was continually nauseated.

August 15. After nine days of suffering, the war came to an end. "OK, the war is over. I'm going to America and I'm going to tell them what happened. This terrible weapon, this bomb must never be dropped again. Such tragedy, such pain, I can't allow it." That thought consumed me. But we were a defeated nation. We had no ships, no airplanes, no food, no clothes, no money. No matter how much I may have wanted to, I couldn't go to America.

Three years later, I got married. Then, I gave birth to a beautiful baby boy, and all our neighbors were happy for me. Eighteen days after his birth, his arms and legs shrank up. Purple spots appeared all over his body. He couldn't drink the milk that was flowing from my breasts. Soon, he stopped breathing. The sad, sad diagnosis was A-bomb disease.

My mother suffered the extremes of horror and pain in both mind and body. She was constantly in and out of the hospital, and finally passed away in 1967 of a gastric ulcer. Immediately after the bombing, my father, a doctor living in Tadanoumi-chō, came to Hiroshima to help with the rescue operation. Later, he got cancer and died. I must have absorbed a large dose of radiation as I walked around searching for my mother. The radiation seems to have collected around my uterus. That's what killed my baby.

June 1982. The Second Special Session of the UN General Assembly Devoted to Disarmament was held in New York. I participated as a representative of survivors. I met two American doctors of engineering, and, to the best of my ability, I was able to tell many Americans about the tragedy of the atomic bombing, the preciousness of life, and the great value of peace.

Now we are in the midst of a global crisis. From the bottom of my heart, I hope that human beings will awaken from the nightmare of nuclear weapons and achieve lasting peace. I will raise my voice and call to every person in the world saying, "We all want to savor our happiness in peace. Let's create a society we can be proud to leave to the children of the 21st century."

Overcoming Agony and Living Courageously

by Taeko Teramae

Introduction

The atomic bomb transformed me in a single instant into a disabled person. Glass fragments shredded my face, and I lost my left eye.

In March of 1945, we second-year students of Shintoku Girls' High School were mobilized to work at one of three locations: the telephone office, the savings office, or Ogawa Factory. Students working in the Ogawa Factory were transferred to the telephone office before the day of the A-bombing. At the time of the bombing, I was working as an operator at the Hiroshima Central Telephone Office, approximately 540 meters from the hypocenter.

August Sixth

The morning was clear, cloudless and fresh. We were all lined up in the corridor carrying our headphones, preparing for the next shift. I was casually gazing up at the blue sky when some object glinted in the sunlight, growing larger and more brilliant as it fell. Puzzled, I asked my friends, "Look, look, what's that?" Then, right in front of my eyes came an explosion of blinding light. That dreadful brilliance seemed enough to melt me. The whole world turned a lightless white; every corner of every shelf just lit up.

Then a huge roar shook the Earth, and all went pitch black. I found myself trapped under something, unable to move. The building made crumbling sounds, and a sickly smell like poison

110

gas filled the air, making it hard to breathe. I vomited. Dust was everywhere, clogging my mouth and eyes. It happened so quickly I was thoroughly disoriented and wondered if I might be dreaming. I continued struggling to get free, and finally I was able to pinch myself. Then I knew. "I'm hurt. This is no dream! The telephone company has been bombed!"

As the crumbling sounds intensified, voices pleading for help arose around me, "Mother, help me! Mother, help me! Mother, I'm hurt!" My despair deepened to terror, and I began chanting a Buddhist prayer in earnest. Suddenly a woman shouted forcefully, "You students, conduct yourselves like students! Be strong!" It was Miss Wakita, our teacher. Our teacher! How that reassuring voice gave hope to all of us! The cries of "Mother!" stopped, and all we could hear were endless grinding sounds of the disintegrating building.

I began to feel something sandy and slimy entering my mouth. Then I noticed that my clothes were wet as well. (I know now that blood from my face wounds was dribbling into my mouth and down onto my clothes.) Desperately I struggled to free myself and finally succeeded. Then, feeling around with my arms and legs, I managed to make my way to the stairs. There, to my amazement, was a jumbled pile of all sorts of people – mobilized students*, girls from the Women's Volunteer Labor Corps, staff members. "I can't go downstairs! What should I do?" I thought. I was at a complete loss. Then I happened to glance out the window by the stair landing and was even more horrified. This was no simple bombing of the telephone office. The morning had turned to blackest night, and the streets were bright with flame. Fire spewed out the windows of every building, the Japan Bank, the Chugoku Power Building, and City Hall, all of them. What had been verdant, large, lush trees were now black-charred wood trunks. Electric poles and their wires were down in the street and the piles of lumber removed from demolished buildings were ablaze with fire.

Thinking, "I've got to get out of here," I jumped from the second-floor window. If I had known that I was missing one eye, that my face had a huge gash, that I in fact looked like a monster, I would have fainted and lost the will to live. As it was I jumped, looked all around me and saw that the city was in flames to the west, south and north. Only Hijiyama Hill to the east looked safe, so I headed off in that direction, carefully avoiding the fallen poles, electric lines, and the burning piles of wood.

On the way I saw only two people, a boy in about the fourth grade of elementary school and a small girl. The girl was naked, darkened with dirt, and apparently unconscious. She may have been dead. Instead of running away, the boy was tugging at her arm, crying and shouting, "You can't die! You can't die!" I deeply regret that I was too intent on escape to spare even a few words of solace for that boy. Moving through those flames without helping others, concentrating only on saving myself, made me feel exactly like an evil sinner wandering through the fires of hell.

I finally reached the banks of the Kyōbashi River. When I looked back at the road I had just walked I was dumbfounded. From one end to another it was a sea of flames now rapidly closing in on the riverbank. I was too terrified to take a second look. People with hair standing straight up, their burnt skin hanging from their bodies, wandered this way and that; some faced the river and screamed. A careful look told me that the Tsurumi Bridge was in flames and that Kyōbashi River was at high tide.

At that point I felt my face begin to swell. Soon, I could barely see. Dread and fear overwhelmed me. One of the telephone office workers approached me with a cigarette, saying, "You look pretty badly hurt. I'm going to put tobacco on your face wound to stop the bleeding, all right?" As he was doing this, my teacher Miss Wakita appeared to take care of me, and I was greatly relieved.

But the flames were bearing down on us, and there was no time to lose. Miss Wakita took my arm and we started to swim

Drawing by an A-bomb Survivor:
People Fleeing from the Burning City (near Kyōbashi Bridge)
(by Kazuhiro Ishizu)

across the river together. When we reached the halfway point I lost my sight completely. Over and over I started to faint and would lose my grasp of my teacher's arm. "Be strong. It's just a little farther. Don't give up!" she urged me, grabbing my arm again, pulling me toward her, and pushing on again. Somehow, we reached the other side. If my teacher had not arrived to help me, I would have been carried off by the current and drowned as were so many of my friends. It was a herculean effort for Miss Wakita to support a wounded student in one arm and swim sidestroke all the way across the river. With all my heart I thank her, my teacher who so selflessly put every ounce of her strength into saving me.

When we finally reached the other bank I was carried in the arms of my teacher up the road to the relief station on Hijiyama Hill. This was a frightful journey with hellish scenes enacted all around us. Voices cried out in anguish, "Help me!" "Mother!" "It hurts!" "Give me water." She described the situation to me as we walked.

The mobilized students who had been demolishing buildings in the Tsurumi Bridge area were from the Hiroshima Prefectural Commercial School (presently, Hiroshima Prefecture Commercial High School); Kōryō Middle School (presently, Kōryō High School); Hiroshima Girls' Commercial School (presently Hiroshima Girls Commercial High School). The heat rays had literally baked their skin. They now lay on the road, writhing in pain. Such cruelty and misery.... Hearing my teacher describe these horrors, I hurried toward the relief station. There we found a long line of people waiting for treatment. My teacher put me in that line and told me to wait. Then she left to reenter that holocaust to try and rescue her other injured students.

The sun reappeared while I was waiting in line, and the intensity of its rays pierced my wounded flesh like knives. Pain flashed through my wounds. Many injured and writhing people were crying out for water, but they did not seem to be receiving any. Before Miss Wakita returned, I received treatment and was taken to Kanawajima along with the other severely injured.

My Family Finds Me

I was desperately waiting for my father, but he did not find me until the fifth day after the A-bombing. As I waited I sensed that many of the people around me were dying, and my fear grew more intense. Waiting only to see my father, one would have expected me to be overjoyed when he came; but the words that came to my lips were a rebuke. "Why didn't you come sooner?"

Just before the atomic bombing my father had been called up to defend the city, but when he learned that Hiroshima had been bombed, he rushed home only to learn from my mother that both his daughters had gone to the city a few days earlier and had disappeared. He searched everywhere, but heard no word of either of us until the next morning (August 7), when he learned that the girls from the First Hiroshima Prefectural Girls' High School (presently, Hiroshima Prefectural Minami High School) were being cared for at Koi Elementary School. He went there in search of my younger sister. He peered closely at the injured girls in hopes of recognizing her; the girls' burned bodies and faces made them strangers even to their loved ones. After three rounds, looking at all the students and reading their name tags, he heard a voice whisper, "Daddy, I'm here." It came from the girl lying at his feet. She was burned everywhere, and her face was so swollen she could not see. She had recognized our father only by his voice. I grieve so when I think of how my sister, destined to die shortly, must have longed to see my father's face. My sister and the other first-year students at the First Hiroshima Prefectural Girls' High School had been helping to demolish buildings at Koami-chō, and every single one of them perished.

Though my father searched intently for me every day, time just dragged by for me, and I wondered angrily, "Why on earth doesn't he come?" Day after day I waited impatiently. Finally, the day came. When we met, I learned the details of my sister's death and the state of the burned-out city.

At Home Again

The seventh day after the bombing I was finally able to return home. I could not see with my own eyes how the city had been burned to the ground. During that first week, before returning, I had remained full of energy, fueled by the desire to stay alive. Perhaps the sense of relief I felt upon going home brought on my sickness. I soon began suffering from high fever, purple blotches all over my skin, bleeding gums, and hair loss. I had all the symptoms of A-bomb disease. Not only did the high fever painfully swell my facial cuts, the rupturing allowed maggots to grow in my wounds. My parents worried constantly. "We got her home alive, but now she too may die."

When visitors came over to express their sympathy, I would overhear them saying, "If only my child had survived – even with severe injuries." I began to wonder just how bad my injuries were. Each time I asked my parents this question, they put me off with "Don't worry." Due to their limitless devotion and care, I was greatly recovered in two months. They even felt confident enough to leave me in the house alone on occasion.

I wanted desperately to see myself in a mirror, but my requests to this effect were met with stony resistance: "You don't need to look into a mirror yet." But one day when I was left alone, I did peek into a mirror – and was thunderstruck. I looked more monstrous than I could ever have imagined. The socket around my missing left eye was hideously sunken in. My face had been gashed all the way from the upper left side to the right edge of my jaw. The tip of my nose had been badly cut. The right side of my face had been torn from eye to ear. Thus, my face was disfigured by two long, jagged scars, like grotesque mountain ranges. "These scars! I didn't know I looked so bad!" Alone in the house I collapsed into tears.

"Hurry up and get well," my parents had constantly urged. They told me that they would lose their minds if they lost both daughters, so I had been determined to regain my health as quickly as possible. But now....

The shock made me keel over. Believing I would have to go through my entire life in that state, I fell into a profound depression. I thought of my sister. Though I pitied her with all my heart, in my mind I often told her, "You were the lucky one." By some miracle I had survived, but I often thought I would be far better off dead.

The Deaths of My Teachers and Friends
In November I learned that a memorial service for our school was to be held at Zenpōji Temple in Koi. Since I had no news of my teachers and friends, I was eager to attend. However, at this

service I received another shock. Miss Wakita, the woman who had saved my life, was dead. Mr. Noguchi and many of my friends had died as well; many were still missing.

Miss Wakita had seemed so energetic after the bombing – how could she be dead? I had arrived wanting more than anything else to thank Miss Wakita for saving me, only to discover that she had died August 30. I was overcome with grief. I wondered what I would have done in Miss Wakita's position that day. When I looked back into that inferno I felt nothing but terror. I could not even look twice. But Miss Wakita, after so bravely rescuing me, had gone back into that holocaust to search for her other students. She was only around twenty years old. How she must have longed to run away! I had survived because she gave her life. I expected nothing but harshness from my life, but when I thought of her suffering, I came to realize that I simply couldn't allow her sacrifice to be wasted. I made up my mind. "I have to be strong!"

Breaking Up

The summer of my twenty-first year I received a love letter.

Near the school I attended after the war were girls' schools like Yūhō High School (formerly, First Hiroshima Prefectural Girls' High School. Presently, Hiroshima Prefectural Minami High School), Hiroshima Girls' School of Commerce, Hijiyama, and Aki. Nearby boys schools included Hiroshima High School, Hiroshima Higher School of Education, National Technical College, and Hiroshima Technical College. During the war, all association between boys and girls had been strictly forbidden. Regulations were eased, however, with the advent of peace. The many students commuting to school on the National Railway Ujina Line had turned the train into a hotbed of budding romance. When I was with my friends, we spent most of our time in romantic gossip. Student life in those days was sweet and full of dreams. Material goods were not as plentiful as today, of course, but I participated fully in student life, and thus was happy. The one facet of life that eluded me was romance – it seemed a prize beyond my reach. Though I had accepted my fate as a girl too ugly to be admired, I still felt terribly lonely. Then one day...... It was like a dream come true.

He wore the square cap of a college boy, so alluring to us girls in those days. He was very active in the campaign for A-bomb survivor relief and had a deep understanding of the atomic bombing. I shed the usual reserve of A-bomb victims, and we shared many happy moments.

The summer of my twenty-fifth year, the mass media turned much of their attention to Hiroshima and the A-bomb victims. They reported the things that survivors were prone to, such as genetic damage, leukemia, white cataracts, infertility, microcephaly, and deformed children. These reports, of course, filled people with fear. For myself, burning with dreams for the future, these reports were a great blow. I had been among those exposed near the hypocenter, and I began to agonize over my fate. I had no desire to visit unhappiness on the man I loved, his family, or our descendants. I told myself to become resigned to my fate. Had I not known the joy of loving and of being loved? Feeling grateful for my many joyful memories, I parted from my love of five years.

Conclusion

There were so many sacrificed – the mobilized students who died in their teens, the bereaved families, those students who survived with terrible handicaps. When I was 26, I wanted to make sure they would never be "forgotten victims of war," so I started a campaign that continues to this day seeking relief for the mobilized students and their families.

Even 53 years since the bombing, most survivors still carry deep wounds in their minds and bodies. We must never again repeat such a tragic evil. The peaceful society we enjoy today was gained at tremendous cost. I hope we will guard it forever and everyone will be able to live a happy life.

Unfortunately, even in supposedly peaceful Japan we are hearing too much lately about suicides caused by bullying at school. What could be sadder?

Please respect your life. Please don't bring sorrow to your parents and others around you.

From the depths of my heart I pray for a peaceful, happy world.

Many Were Sacrificed to Attain Today's Peace

by Noriko Ueda

August 6 (Monday) Clear

My sister and I were cheerful first and second year students going to the First Hiroshima Prefectural Girls' High School every day, dressed in *monpe* (work pants) and wooden clogs. My grade, the second year students, had been mobilized for the war effort in mid-July and formed into three groups to work at the Hiroshima Airport Company, Hiroshima Printing Company, and the Army Clothing Depot. I was assigned to the printing company in Kan'on-machi. Every day I picked type and did tracing. On August 6, seen to the door by our mother, we left together. I headed for Hiroshima Printing as usual, and my sister was going for the first time to the Dobashi area to clear away debris at demolished building sites. My sister had happily asked for some money from our mother the night before. She wanted to have a friend in Kaita buy a straw hat for her.

I arrived at the factory at about 8 o'clock. I left my two bags in the assigned room, took up a wooden rifle, and ran to the northwest corner of the yard of the Second Municipal National School. While we were lined up in the school yard for morning assembly, an orange light suddenly surged across the sky. I thought, "the whole world is dyed orange," and at the same time all sound seemed to cease. When I recovered my senses I stuck my thumbs in my ears, covered my eyes tightly with the other four fingers, and lay face down on the ground. Frequent drills had ingrained this protective posture deeply in all of us. Three of my friends at the end of the line were burned instantly.

Fortunately, most of us were in the shadow of the school building and were not injured.

It seemed to us that a bomb had fallen on the school building. We knew nothing about atomic bombs or anything like that. We all returned to the factory and, pulling our bags from the damaged building, put them over our shoulders. Then we ran back to the school to take refuge in the air-raid shelter in the school grounds. My lunch was in one of my bags. The other was called an emergency bag and contained first aid supplies and emergency rations. The rations included roasted rice and soy beans, and sugar candy in a tea canister. Under normal conditions, we were not allowed to eat this food no matter how hungry we were. Some injured elementary students were placed in the air-raid shelter, and we were told, "Get out of the way. The injured get treatment first." Many of people of the neighborhood took refuge in the school yard. I was wandering there aimlessly when black rain began to fall. It was so hot I thought, "It's cooler to get wet," but that rain stained our uniforms black. The rain stopped and just before noon, I think, we were told to take refuge with our teacher in the hills near Koi. As we walked on and on toward the west, we saw that the buildings were dreadfully damaged. We grew extremely nervous and continued our flight as fast as we could, careful not to lose sight of the back of the student in front to keep from getting lost, and trying not to look at those so appallingly injured they no longer looked human. A frightfully large number of injured and uninjured were fleeing to the west.

When we came to the river, the water was at high tide. We squatted in a group around the trees under the bank to wait for the tide to recede. People burnt to tatters came fleeing one after another to where we were and squatted down, just like us. Saying, "Let's help them," we brought out our first-aid supplies and began to give them first aid. Our teacher had taught us some simple first-aid procedures, and we spread the medicine on enthusiastically. There was an old man I cannot forget to this day. His whole body was burned. I think he was almost entirely unclothed. He came hesitantly to my side, saying anxiously, "I came early this morning from Ōtake on an errand to the Hiroshima Prefectural Office, but look what happened to me. I want to hurry home as soon as I can, but I wonder if the train is running at Koi Station." I told him that we would cross the river when the tide went down to take refuge in the hills at Koi, "Why don't you come along with us." "Yes, please take me with you" he said weakly, and crouched at my feet. With my dirty hands, I spread medicine on his burns.

Soon, the medicine was gone. Then, agreeing that it was acceptable to eat them today, we ate our emergency rations. Everyone thought the day constituted a crisis, so we brought out the food and shared it among us. It was a time in which

Drawing by an A-bomb Survivor:
Burned survivors in a truck at Koi Station.   (by Toshiko Kihara)

everyone had to help each other to survive. My mother had packed a box of ten Morinaga Milk Caramels along with the roasted rice and soy beans in my bag. They were melted, but I shared them among the ten of us.

When the water receded we helped each other across the river. We parted with the old man at Koi Station. He squatted down where he was and rested, unmoving with his head hanging. We walked toward the hills in a strange, silent procession. When passing Koi National School, which had been turned into a relief station, we learned that the first-year students of our school had taken refuge there, and that my sister's teacher, Ms. Mitsutani, had collapsed under the eaves of a house nearby. I had thought until then that only we second and third-year students mobilized at the printing factory had been hit. Learning that the first year students working at clearing up the demolished buildings had also been hit, I realized for the first time that something really terrible had happened that day. My anxiety gradually turned to fear. Feeling nothing but this fear, I allowed myself to be herded along with the others. The teacher told us all to go to a printing plant in the hills, then went back to the relief station with five or six third year students to help the first-year students and Ms. Mitsutani. My friends pushed my shoulder, urging me to go with the teacher to look for my sister, but I was afraid to go back. I was so scared that my legs wouldn't move. I didn't return to look for my sister, Mutsuko, who is missing to this day. I still wonder where and how she died. I agonize to this day wondering why I didn't go to the relief station to search for her, why I didn't check to see if she was there. I'm sure I will always regret that. I remember telling myself, 14 at the time, that "At least my family must be all right. Surely they did their best and somehow escaped to some safe place."

At the relief station, those who were able to do so reported their address, name, and blood type, which were recorded. Many were too badly injured to give this information. When they died, they were cremated right there in a great pit in the school yard. People suffering terrible burns arrived in an unending stream until they seemed to overflow the school. They were so badly burned they seemed changed into other people; their own brothers and sisters and parents could not recognize them. It was a scene beyond expression by words or drawings or photographs. It was a day I hate to recall.

August 7th (Tuesday) Clear

Last night I ate half a rice ball that someone gave me.

Anxiously calling, "Father!" "Mother!" we all watched from the hill as Hiroshima continued to burn. At dawn, the teacher said, "Last night I sent a messenger to our school, but the fires were so furious he couldn't get near it. He came back right away. The students and teachers are all dead by this morning." I lost awareness for a time. Benumbed, I looked at things without seeing them.

There was nothing to eat. We were dismissed at that point, and I thought I would go home. On the way, some benefactor put a piece of hardtack on my palm, which I nibbled as I walked. There were many dead bodies floating in the river. Some were tied with straw rope so they wouldn't float away. They stank very badly. Someone trapped under a collapsed chimney had been burned almost entirely to white bones.

I don't want to talk about the scenes burned into my eyes that day, but I believe I must speak. The iron streetcar bridge was still standing, so I crossed it. Staggering with fatigue, I stopped at the printing factory. A factory worker near the broken building wrote a disaster certificate for me. When I was walking home, I came upon an army truck. A soldier was calling out news of people with a megaphone from the bed of the truck. I was very fortunate to hear news of my father and mother in this way. Joyfully, I went immediately to take refuge where they were. Until then, I had lost all human feelings. I believe that I regained my human nature in the instant I heard news of my family.

Not to care, to be without sensation in such a horrible situation is inhuman. Such a terrible thing must never happen again. I was 14 at the time and will be gone before long, but I hope the next generations of young people will hear the stories of as many survivors as possible. I earnestly hope that my story will be meaningful to young people like you and that you will make good use of it in nurturing your own children. In that war many ordinary people leading ordinary lives were instantly sacrificed in Hiroshima and Nagasaki to the atomic bombs. So many ordinary people were also killed by B-29 bombings in cities all over the country. There are victims of the war throughout Japan and survivors of that time near to everyone. I want young people to hear as many stories as possible from them and use that knowledge to guide the generations to come. Nothing is more dangerous than ignorance. I want everyone to study many things, to learn many things, and to become people who can judge situations for themselves and say, "This is wrong!"

My sister left a diary with no entry for August 6. The last entry begins, "August 5 (Sunday) Clear," and ends, "...today was a really wonderful day." Even in such terrible times, many children were cheerful and patient. "We won't want anything until we win," they said, and they died. I want you to know that there were countless children like that. I hope you can understand that the lives we live today are built on the lives they lost.

The Unspeakable Tragedy of that Day

by Miyoko Watanabe

August 6, 1945. That morning was bright and clear. The mid-summer sun was shining strongly. A yellow air-raid warning was lifted, and we all breathed a little easier. My house was near Miyuki Bridge, 2.3 kilometers southeast of the hypocenter.

I had been mobilized, but I had the day off because the factory to which I was assigned shut down on the first Monday of each month to avoid using electricity. I left home for the post office at Miyuki Bridge. On the way, I decided the sun was so intense I should go home and get a parasol. I was leaving the house again and had just opened the parasol when I was bathed in a powerful flash.

It was like the magnesium flash of a camera, but with some yellow or orange mixed in and hundreds of times brighter. I thought a bomb had fallen on the gas tank across the river, causing it to explode. I ran instantly into my house and lay face down in the posture we had been taught to take in air raids. I heard some extremely odd shaking and crashing noises. Filled with fear, I opened my eyes and saw that the west wall of my house had fallen down. I could see right into our factory in back of the house. Even as I was thinking, "I survived," I was filled with a terrible dread. When I went out side, the sky that had been so blue moments before was dark as evening. An odd smell was in the air that I could not describe.

When I came fully to myself, I looked toward the house wondering what had happened to my mother. I found her with her hair a mess and standing on end. Her lips were split and her face was covered with blood from her head. She was a terrible sight. My younger brother's white *kimono* was stained bright red, and he was staggering around. I said, "Are you alright?" to my brother, and my mother answered. "That's my blood. The boy's not injured." When I looked at my mother again I saw blood spurting from her right wrist. I rushed to get some medicine from our emergency kit that would stop the bleeding. I put it on her face and stopped the bleeding from her arm with a tourniquet. My older brother and two men from our factory put her on a stretcher and took her to the Hiroshima Army Mutual Aid Hospital. They got her dangling lip, jaw, and shoulder sewed up without any anesthetic. Because her wrist had already received some first aid, it wasn't treated. That might be why it took so long to heal. Even now her index and middle fingers don't move properly.

Her index finger began to rot above the first joint and grew a black fingernail. After a week, I removed the stitches from her wounds. Because the numbness in her lip and jaw continued, I looked inside her mouth and found some glass fragments. They were about the size of the nail on my little finger. We found five of them. My mother said she wasn't feeling well so we should just stop, but I took some tweezers and looked around for more. I found two more smaller pieces. This was a frightening reminder of the power of that blast.

The tragic conditions in our area right after the bombing are still etched in my mind. I saw a woman who had been nursing her baby lying dead on her house near the riverbank. It was obvious that she bled to death when a glass fragment carried by the blast slit her left carotid artery. In her blood-covered arms, the baby, not knowing his mother was dead, was still sucking innocently at her breast. That scene still comes back to me vividly.

After a while I became aware of blood flowing from my little finger, and I suddenly felt intense pain. I had no idea what to do, so I washed it in water from the pump and put medicine on it. Then I ran into the air-raid shelter with my younger brother. Even today, my little finger remains small and bent and hurts when I'm in bad condition. Inside the shelter, nothing was normal. There was so much groaning. A horrible odor struck my nose, making me instantly nauseated. Then I noticed a little boy about one-and-a-half with his internal organs bursting out of his body. He breathed his last as his mother held him gazing into his white face. A beautiful little girl about five with long hair lay there bleeding profusely. She died, too.

As I left the shelter, I saw a boy about junior high age burned and without hair except on the top of his head where he had been wearing a combat cap. He staggered along like a ghost with both hands held out in front of him. The skin on his cheeks had burst open and was dangling down. He was horribly burned and walking barefoot saying, "Water please! I'm so hot! I'm burning!" Japan's military education taught boys never to say anything weak or feminine. Even though he was mortally burned, he never said, "Help me!"

Many female students had their clothes burned to tatters. The skin was peeling off and hanging from the tips of their fingers. My father came home burned over his entire body. We were terribly shocked. I was still convinced that a bomb had fallen on our factory behind our house, so I couldn't believe that my father was so burned. He had been doing building demolition work near the Hiroshima Red Cross Hospital, which was 1.5 kilometers from the hypocenter. I just couldn't understand why he, too, was so burned. I went into our broken house and found some cooking oil to put on his burns. Father was worried about mother, so he walked with steady steps to the Hiroshima Army Mutual Aid Hospital. So many people with burns approached me that I was out of oil in no time.

Father came home with mother. He had a little mercurochrome on him, but there were so many burn victims even the hospital had run out of medicine. The *futon* in the stretcher my mother was carried in were soaked and sticky with dried blood. Mother's fingers were still covered with congealing blood. We washed them with water from the pump and at last they started to move a little. Her toes were the same, and the *monpe* (work pants) she was wearing were also dried hard. Later, when we soaked them overnight in water, the water quickly turned bright red. We washed them over and over, but every time the water turned red with blood.

A soldier said, "There's a first-aid station near Miyuki Bridge. Injured people should go there." Father went, and was taken directly on to Ninoshima Island. Why did we let our badly burned father go there by himself? I ached with regret.

On August 8, we brought our father home from Ninoshima. Flies were drawn by his white medicine and the pus from his burns, and it was hard to keep them away. Father kept saying, "Give me water." But we had heard that if a burn victim drank water he would die, so we gave him only about a small cup a few times a day. We kept water from him because we wanted him to live. Looking back, my heart still fills with regret.

On the day Japan surrendered, he commented weakly, "So Japan lost...." The following evening he said, "I'm cold," and died, all too quickly. Fifty-three years later, the sorrow I feel about his death has just increased. At the time, we saw such a tremendous amount of death our nerves were numbed.

The center of the city was burning, covered with black smoke. A man I knew who worked at Dentetsu (Hiroshima Electric Railway Co., Ltd., 1.9 kilometers from the hypocenter) came to our house. He told me in tears how he had failed to save his younger sister and was forced to leave her behind. "The bomb fell right on Dentetsu. The back of my head was injured. I wanted to go to the Hiroshima Red Cross Hospital (1.5 kilometers from the hypocenter), but it was burning, so I tried to go home. I got to my house in Takanobashi (1.1 kilometer from the hypocenter) by dodging through the fire. My house was flattened. I called my sister's name. She said, 'Help me! Call the Civilian Guard!' Black smoke around us was already turning to

Drawing by an A-bomb survivor:
Person Calling for Help from Collapsed, Burning Houses

(by Kanichi Itō)

flame. Soon it was bearing down on us. Not knowing what to do, I struggled to remove the rubble. It got hotter and hotter. Finally, I just couldn't stand the heat. 'I'm sorry. Please forgive me,' I said and I left. I could hardly tear myself away. I kept hearing her say, 'You watched me die and didn't do anything. You're a demon.' I did a cruel thing." He was sobbing as he finished his story. All of those who left burning homes and survived have lived, to some extent, with the secret feeling of having done something terribly cruel.

We could not stay where we were. Putting my younger brother and my mother, who had come back from the Hiroshima Army Mutual Aid Hospital, onto a handcart, we fled to the house of an acquaintance in Tanna. I will never forget the horrible scenes I saw on the way.

The post office was completely collapsed, and an army horse was lying dead on its back. Crowds of people were squatting at the foot of Miyuki Bridge. They were weakly calling, "Water, water please." The bridge railing had been blown into the river by the blast. I saw soldiers cremating a mountain of corpses. For some reason, I looked at all those corpses without the feeling I have now about the sanctity of life. We were bombed with such suddenness. So many people had died. Maybe we had lost the ability to feel.

Beginning about the end of August, I had terrible diarrhea and blood in my stools. I lost some of my hair. We had no medicine, so I boiled some wild herbs and drank the tea. Somehow, I managed to survive, but the damage of the bomb lasted far beyond that August. Many who came into the area later to search for their children or brothers or sisters would suddenly develop a high fever, go a little crazy, get purple spots on their skin, and, one after the next, they would collapse and die. There were thousands of cases like that.

Ten years after the bombing, I developed anemia and a loss of liver function. I suffered terribly with that for four or five years. An unsightly stain peculiar to loss of liver function spread over my face. Every time I brushed my teeth, my gums would bleed. I lived in continual fear. Thankfully, I have hung on until today. Eighteen years after the bombing, my older brother got leukemia and died following a painful struggle. At the time, he had been working in the Hiroshima Prefectural District Lumber Control Corporation in what is now the A-bomb Dome. That day, his work day was delayed for one hour, so he was at home and his life was spared. But after the 9th, not knowing that the hypocenter was dangerously contaminated with radiation, he went to his office repeatedly to dig through the rubble and look for belongings of the dead. In 1947 he got a lung infection. The next year he got stomatitis. He was continually in and out of the Hiroshima Red Cross Hospital. It never occurred to us that his illnesses were caused by the bomb. My mother would say,

"You're weak. You're a disease warehouse." I'm sure he suffered a great deal from her criticism. He really had radiation right into the marrow of his bones. After he was cremated we found that his bones were unusually light and porous. They were empty like pumice, and reddish brown like bricks, with a touch of black. When we touched them, they just crumbled immediately. When I tried to hold them, they slipped right through my fingers like sand. They were so strange. In my brother's bones I saw vividly and clearly the true horror of nuclear weapons.

The word "Hiroshima" is known around the world. Those who somehow managed to survive in that city of death have lived ever since with aftereffects and anxiety about their health. They have battled continually with the demon of disease. Today's peace is built on the sacrifices of war victims the world over. Wars are the worst possible misfortune. I only hope that we will have the tenderness of heart to feel the pain of others as our own. The voice of Hiroshima is calling for lasting peace. I hope the tiny ripples we make now will grow someday into a giant wave. Nuclear weapons are inhumane. I will continue to tell the world from Hiroshima that human beings and nuclear weapons cannot coexist indefinitely, and I will continue to pray for the realization of permanent, genuine world peace.

Everyone in My Department Is Dead

by Rikio Yamane

I am profoundly aware of the sanctity of life and the joy of peace. When I see my friends and colleagues departing this world for the next, I feel, deep in my heart, that "all is transient, nothing is permanent." Some of those friends are atomic bomb survivors departing from lives of great suffering. The epitaph engraved on the Cenotaph for the A-bomb Victims in Peace Memorial Park reads, "Let All The Souls Here Rest In Peace; For We Shall Not Repeat The Evil." The Peace Memorial Ceremony on August sixth every year commemorates a day the citizens of Hiroshima will never forget. An old proverb says, "Get new lessons by studying the old." For this reason, I have determined to recall the atomic bombing and record the cruel tragedy of that time.

Though forty-five years have passed since the end of the war, I still shudder with horror when I recall the day the atomic bomb fell. Sometimes I wonder at how I have remained alive all this time. At the time, I was a physical education officer for the Hiroshima city government – all the other members of that department have since died. I lived two kilometers south of the hypocenter in Minamimachi, near the foot of Miyukibashi, Hiroshima's longest bridge. The air-raid warning for the previous night had been lifted, and I prepared for August sixth with a sense of relief. It was a midsummer day, and the sun was shining brilliantly. Seven or eight members of the neighborhood association had gathered, and we were discussing our rations. (Shortages of all kinds had forced rationing of food and other daily necessities.) Suddenly one of the group shouted, "Look, a B-29!" We looked where he was pointing and saw a lone enemy plane, glinting silver in the sun, heading north in the southern sky.

Aah! Just at that instant a ray of light blazed across the sky. I felt as if something had been thrown into my eyes. My face stung. I instinctively sensed a terrible disaster and jumped back into the house. Immediately, the house shook as if in an earthquake. The ceiling fell and debris rained down. Roof tiles clattered to the ground. Everything around me turned pitch black. I groped my way through the house and finally clawed my way out a tiny window in the back. Close by was the river, and I struggled to get to its banks. I stood there thoroughly stunned, and gradually, as if a fog were lifting, the area around me stood revealed. I saw that Miyuki Bridge, immediately in front of me, had lost all its parapets. Those on the far side were lying flat, torn from their foundations. The nearside parapets had completely disappeared, probably into the river. Electric poles had also been felled, and the wires lay tangled like some huge spider's web. That moment was so silent, so incredibly silent. I felt utterly strange, and wondered what could possibly have happened. For a while I just stood there at the foot of the bridge.

Soon I found myself watching, like some hellish marathon, a procession of ghastly, inhuman figures fleeing from the city. Their burned skin had peeled and was dangling in shreds. Shirts had been ripped to tatters and appeared more like night garments. It was impossible even to differentiate males from females. Half naked, half dead, all were pushing forward as one, begging to be rescued. With a start, I came to myself. Realizing the horror of the situation I rushed frantically to the police box at Minamimachi. (At that time, the city was using police boxes as information relay stations.) The policeman on guard there looked grotesque, like a demon. His mouth was ripped open clear back through his cheeks. Spitting blood, he was using a towel to bind up his jaw. He could not speak for the pain and seemed on the verge of collapse. I assumed his cheeks had been torn open by the force of the blast.

I felt I could not stop and take care of this one man, so I directed him to the Hakuai Clinic, then ran off to the Hiroshima Red Cross Hospital for help. On the way, I passed Senda Park where I saw a half-naked woman about thirty years of age. When I looked more closely I saw a newborn babe with the umbilical cord still attached. In amazement I called to her, "Who are you? What is your name? Where do you live?" She could not answer. After a while she drew a painful breath, turned toward me, put her hands together as if in prayer, and gasped, "Please, just save the baby. Please help my child." Ignoring her own pain, she continued to cry for me to help the baby.

Watching her, I was struck by the power and sanctity of a mother's love and broke down in tears. Even as she was losing consciousness this woman was forgetting her own suffering, clasping her hands together in prayer for her newborn baby. I saw this woman as the Merciful Mother Kannon, *Jibo Kannon* (Kannon is a bodhisattva who symbolizes the great compassion of Buddha), and my heart was moved to the point of pain. Japanese women in those days were so magnificent and strong, true women of Japan.

But there was absolutely nothing I could do. All I could think of was finding a doctor for her, so I ran as quickly as possible to the Hiroshima Red Cross Hospital. On the way I saw a horse collapsed and writhing on the ground. I saw people who had jumped into a water tank nearby, piled on top of one another, groaning in agony. These were the cruel scenes of a hell beyond words, absolutely unimaginable in this world.

Finally I arrived at the hospital and entered, expecting to find some sort of relief work in progress. Instead, it was more of the same horror. The entire floor was covered with glass splinters, so it felt more like a surface of sand than of cement. Everyone was injured; it was impossible to differentiate the doctors from the patients. The nurses, their uniforms black and shredded, were rushing back and forth in indecision, unable to really help anyone. It was as if I had just walked into a haunted house. There was no help to be found there, so I left and headed for a nearby government office. But that building was on fire, tongues of flame licking viciously out the open windows. At a loss, I began retracing my steps. When I returned to the place where I had seen the woman and newborn babe, they were gone. Perhaps they had been hauled away; two precious lives undoubtedly lost.

As I walked along I decided to go to Minami Elementary School. I thought I might help set up a relief station there. On my way I put out flames darting from the houses along the road. I arrived at the school to find it collapsed, with people groaning here and there. The army's Akatsuki Corps was stationed in the school gymnasium, but the road do it was blocked; again, there was nothing I could do, so I left.

Tired in mind and body I arrived back at my house just after 3:00 p.m. None of the men who had been doing the rationing* that morning were anywhere to be seen. My wife and two-year-old child had been unable to do anything but wait anxiously for my return. When my wife saw me, she suddenly burst into tears. She told me there was something hanging from my throat and, as I touched it, I found that it was soft. When I pulled it away I realized that a layer of skin had peeled from my face and was hanging from my neck. Stretching in out I could see the holes for my mouth, nose and eyes. I also had two large blisters on my hands. (Today my only keloids are on my throat, which is rough like a bear's. My face, thanks to treatment, has returned to normal.)

Since our house had collapsed and we had no place to stay, we decided to head that evening for my hometown Yae in Yamagata County (now called Chiyodachō). Electric poles were down everywhere and the lines were all over the road, so we picked our way carefully along Hijiyama Hill and, after great effort, finally arrived at Hiroshima Station. I felt we had done remarkably well to get that far. Hiroshima Station was burning like a steel furnace, the surrounding streets flaming like waves in a sea of fire. Carrying our baby in our arms we fled for our lives. When we got to Nikitsu Shrine we saw a freight train on its side; in some cars horses and cows were piled on each other and suffering terribly. Corpses were strewn all around the area. No greater horror is imaginable. I cannot describe in mere words the pitiful state of the many suffering victims begging for water. It was absolutely hell, a living hell.

By the time we had followed the river to Ushita, the warehouse of the Engineering Corps* was completely ablaze. The entire city of Hiroshima appeared to be one gigantic conflagration – a sea of fire, a city of fire. The sun was beginning to set. Fewer people were on the streets. Exhausted and dragging our legs

Drawing by an A-bomb Survivor:
Fleeing with my wife and child on a bicycle (west of Nikitsu Shrine)
(by Rikio Yamane)

wearily, we finally made it to Hesaka. There we decided to spend the night in a grove of low, bushy bamboo trees growing along the river. I awoke during the night and looked out toward the sky over Hiroshima. The city was still completely engulfed in flames, and I was overcome with loneliness.

The summer dawn came early. When I awoke I noticed a woman standing dejected and lost in the mist shrouding the reeds at the water's edge. I called out, "Hey!"

"Yes?" she answered, turning around to look at me. I felt waves of shock wrenching my innards. Even my scream caught in my throat. Her right eye was bulging out, and her left eyeball was hanging monstrously down her cheek. Her lips were swollen, and her face, a sickly blackish-blue, seemed twice its normal size. A single night had done this to my wife. She looked like an evil ghost from some sort of play. She had changed so utterly I found myself wishing she would simply die. I pounded my chest and screamed, "Who did this to her? Give me back my wife! Put her back the way she was!" I was crying as I shouted. Then it was over. "Let's go home. Let's go home," I murmured. With my eyes closed I grabbed her by the hand. In this manner, the child on her back, we set out once again.

Up river we came to a ford and boarded the ferry. The ferryman burst into tears, "You poor people, you poor people." He cried as he rowed us across to the other side. From there we dragged ourselves two kilometers to the town of Kabe. An ancient saying goes, "Like finding Buddha in Hell," which was exactly how we felt when the bus pulled in just as we arrived. We joined the ten or so injured people on board and rode all the way to my home town. (Buses in those days burned charcoal.)

My parents and two of our children, a son in fifth and a daughter in second grade of elementary school, had been evacuated to this village earlier. We called to our children when we arrived, but when they saw us they cried, "Ghosts! They're ghosts!" and hid behind pillars, peeping out at us fearfully. My parents came out and ran to embrace us. "Who did this to you? I hate them! I hate America! Doing this to my last child...." (My two younger brothers had already died in the war. One was killed in the battle of Xúzhōu in China; the other, a member of the Kumagaya Air Regiment, was dispatched to replace the commanding officer of the Endō Division in New Guinea, where he too was killed.)

My father, crying and shouting loudly, stomped the ground over and over as if he had gone mad. I was so grateful for his feeling for me; I was overjoyed to see him. I can still feel the warmth of his embrace.

One of our relatives was a doctor, and we went to see him every day. My parents spread a straw mat and some cushions on a wood cart (which they used for hauling wood down from the mountains), then Father pulled and Mother pushed all the way to the doctor's office. While we were there, the doctor would apply some sort of oil to our skin, then wrap our faces in cloth bandages, leaving openings for nose, eyes, and mouth. Gauze such as we have now were rare, so we ripped up summer kimonos and took them to the hospital for the doctor to use for our bandages. Returning home, the summer heat would dry the blood and pus on our faces, causing the new skin to stick to the cloth. When the tightness became too painful, my mother would stay up all night squeezing cucumber and tomato juice and dripping it onto our bandages. These wounds were excruciating; we suffered terribly. Day after day we went to the doctor to get our bandages changed and – oh, the pain! The continual peeling off of cloth stuck to us with blood and pus was truly unbearable. I have heard it said that this process is similar to tearing away living flesh, and that was the sensation exactly. So much suffering... but we endured.

The treatment did gradually begin to have an effect, but then, just after the relief of having three glass fragments removed from my face, our hair started to fall out. Watching my wife cry as she looked into the mirror to comb what was left of her hair, I felt such intense sadness and resentment. Finally she lost all of it. She looked like an entirely different person. When she cried to me, begging, "I want to die! Just let me die!" I struggled with myself for a while. But the passing of time, the warm nursing of my parents, and our own mental strength began to rekindle our will to live. One year, two years – somehow our bodies returned to normal. Looking back, our recovery seems nothing short of miraculous.

That suffering is over, and we have returned safely from the "Realm of Death." We literally stood at the crossroads, and I am astonished at having survived this long. I cannot but feel overwhelmingly grateful for the intangible power of human compassion and the parental love that nurtured the happiness we feel today.

The war ended. Japan has overcome the bitter trials of surrender to build an age of peace and affluence no one then could have imagined. Hiroshima has been reborn a city of water and greenery, working to become an "international city of peace and culture." Here is the starting point for world peace, and we are crying to the world with all our might to abolish the threat of nuclear war.

At the request of the Hiroshima Peace Culture Foundation, I meet and talk to some of the many children who visit Hiroshima on their school trips. The meaning of my life now lies in telling these children, the ones who will inherit the burdens and responsibilities of the next century, of the horrors of nuclear war, the reality of the atomic bomb, the sanctity of peace, the power of the life force, and the importance of being grateful for what we have.

Conveying the Spirit of Hiroshima to the Entire World

by Michiko Yamaoka

My youth will never return, but vivid images of August 6, 1945, still live in my mind. When I think of that experience and all the friends I lost, even now I tremble with grief and anger.

I was 15 years old, a third-year student at a girls' high school, but as a mobilized student, I commuted daily from my house to work at the Hiroshima Central Telephone Office (belonging to what is now NTT). The office was 540 meters from the hypocenter.

My father died when I was three, so my mother and I lived alone. My mother enjoyed watching me grow up. She supported me by herself until she died in February 1980.

The sky dawned cloudless blue on August 6. Hiroshima, the "city of water" was very beautiful. I was unusually reluctant to leave for work that day, but I pulled myself together and started for work a little before 8:00. My younger cousins, who had come to our house from the countryside, left a little before me for the Hiroshima Red Cross Hospital. We still don't know where they died or what happened to them. We never even found their bones.

I left saying, "See you tonight," as usual.

"The B29's are gone, but be careful," my mother called after me as I hurried away from the house. Walking down a road about 800 meters from the hypocenter, I heard the roar of a B29. "How strange," I thought. "The all-clear just sounded." Just as I shaded my eyes with my hand to look up in the sky, there was a yellow-blue flash like the magnesium flash of a camera. I remember rising into the air before my consciousness faded. Thinking, "I've been bombed," I shouted in my heart, "Goodbye, Mother!"

I don't know how long I was unconscious – maybe 10 or 20 minutes. A child's screams brought me back. I was buried under wreckage and couldn't move. Everything was black. "Someone help me! Mother help me!" I shouted over and over.

Then I heard my mother calling my name. "Michiko, Michiko!"

"Mother, I'm here, I'm here!" I called from beneath the wreckage. She couldn't see me. Only my feet were sticking out.

She continued to shout, "Michiko, where are you? Michiko!" but she couldn't find me. I began to lose hope.

I heard voices in the vicinity shouting, "Lady, the fire's coming! Run for your life!" I could hear fire crackling. Thinking it was over for me, I closed my eyes.

"Soldier, please help me! My daughter is trapped under here." She had finally found me. "Soldier, please hurry and get this wreckage off of her!" she shouted emphatically. Finally, I was able to crawl out from under the debris. I could already feel that my face was blown up like a balloon.

Looking around, I held my breath. This wasn't the world I knew – it was a living hell. A person without a head, a dazed woman cradling a dead infant, a child whose whole body was burnt slippery, a corpse with internal organs pouring out. Lines of completely naked people. Carnage was everywhere. The images are still imprinted on my mind, and whenever I recall them, I cannot stop the tears. In 53 years since the bombing, I have never been able to eat sausages – they remind me of the internal organs I saw that day.

My mother told me to seek refuge on Hijiyama Hill, and we parted. I walked toward Hijiyama alone. My mother had put all else aside to come after me. Now she returned to the house to see about her uncle and aunts, whom she had left there. It was some relief to know that, though injured, they had survived.

As I fled, I encountered a friend. I called her name, but she didn't recognize me. "Who are you?" she asked.

"Michiko Yamaoka." She couldn't believe the person with the swollen, strange face was me. On learning that I was altered beyond recognition, I was filled with grief. This was when I first felt the stinging pain and heat of my burns.

Hijiyama Hill was crowded with burn victims. I lay down and someone applied *tempura* oil to my burns. My mother found me again, and I forgot my pain when we embraced. After some time, since I was one of the seriously injured, I was transported by boat to a relief station outside the city. Injured people in the boat died one after another. Thinking, "Will I be the next to go?" I closed my eyes and prayed.

I groaned, "Soldier, give me water."

Drawing by an A-bomb survivor:
The piteous condition of middle school students (Hijiyama Hill)
(by Toshifumi Gotō)

"I'll give you water," he scolded, "if you want to die." Unable to watch me suffer so, my mother secretly gave me a little water. It may have been that water that drastically worsened my condition. I lost all the hair on my head, my urine and stools turned bloody, and I nearly died. Somehow I survived, but my face had changed. Keloids pushed out of the skin, distorting my features. I closeted myself at home, refusing to go out and be seen. I lost all hope for the future. If I had been alone, I probably would have killed myself. But my mother was always with me, continuing to work for my sake though she was hospitalized repeatedly herself. I couldn't die.

In May 1955, thanks to the good will of many Americans and Japanese, I was given the chance to travel to the US for plastic surgery. Behind my back some murmured, "She's going to the very country that dropped the bomb. They'll probably kill her!" But I was so desperate to regain my former appearance that I believed in those who were trying to help. I underwent a total of 27 operations. Though I was in continual pain I endured, clinging to a thread of hope. I still often think, "If only there had been no war," or "If only the atomic bomb hadn't been dropped."

I finally understood that it was wrong to lock myself in a dark shell forever. I broke my silence of nearly 20 years and began to talk about my A-bomb experience to younger generations who have never known war. To prevent more victims, I will appeal for the abolition of nuclear weapons as long as I have breath. The steeper the road to abolition, the louder I will raise my voice to help spread the spirit of Hiroshima – the pursuit of peace. Never believe that we are powerless. Peace will come through the accumulation of individual efforts. My heart's deepest desire is the abolition of nuclear weapons and genuine peace on Earth.

Chapter 3

Foreign Atomic Bomb Victims

Foreign Atomic Bomb Victims

by Toshiko Uehara

Assistant Director
Proofreading Group
Editorial Department
Chūgoku Shimbun Newspaper
Company

Introduction

Among the victims of the atomic bomb that fell on Hiroshima on August 6, 1945, were Koreans, Chinese, Americans, White Russians, Germans, Indonesians, and Malaysians as well as Japanese-Americans raised in America. They were living in and around Hiroshima as students, ordinary residents, missionaries, soldiers and military-related personnel; many, in addition, were forced to be there, either as prisoners or conscript laborers. The atomic bomb exploded above a diversity of people.

The issue of foreign victims of the atomic bombing was hardly touched for some time after the war. Examining the reasons that so many foreigners were present at this time, we are confronted with the fact that many were the victims of Japan's colonial invasions. During the more than forty years since the war, attempts have been made to clarify the fate of these foreign victims and survivors, but the findings are still largely estimates.

The vast majority of foreign survivors were Koreans, and most of them returned after the war to their homelands, either the Republic of Korea (South Korea) or the Democratic People's Republic of Korea (North Korea). Other survivors returned or emigrated to China, America, Canada, and South America.

Koreans
[Before the Bombing]

Koreans were in Hiroshima at the time of the atomic bombing because of the "Japan-Korea Annexation Treaty" of 1910 and the subsequent rapid colonization of Korea by Japan. After signing the treaty, Japan undertook a full-scale land survey, and Korean land with complicated ownership determined by the old, feudalistic system was seized by Japan. As a result, many Koreans were driven from the land of their ancestors and forced to seek a living in Japan or northeast China (then Manchuria).

Table 1 shows the population of Koreans in Japan and in Hiroshima Prefecture from 1910 to 1920. Up to the year 1916, that population was less than 100, but it jumped dramatically the following year. It temporarily dwindled in 1919 – 20 when the Government-General of Korea (Japanese government in Korea), fearful of the influence of the "March 1 Independence Movement" of 1919, introduced a system of travel restrictions. But with the implementation in 1920 of the Rice Production Increase Plan, land confiscation increased, and emigration to Japan jumped again. When travel to Japan was freed in 1922, the number of Koreans in Japan continued to increase.

In the mid - 1920s, the economic collapse of Korean farms and villages due to the worldwide depression, plus the need in Japan for cheap labor brought about by military-demand-driven inflation, and various other factors, further stimulated Korean emigration to Japan.

After the Manchurian Incident of 1931, Japan, headed toward war, began pressing for the unification of the homeland and Korea. Korean forced-labor programs began in 1939, the year after the National Mobilization Law was passed. These programs first took the form of "recruiting" by personnel departments of private companies. From 1942 on, however, agencies of the Government-General of Korea were "encouraging" workers to come to Japan, and this escalated in 1944 into an outright labor draft that mobilized Korean workers. During this period,

as can be seen in Table 2, the Korean population in Hiroshima
Prefecture increased drastically, mushrooming to 81,863 by the

Table 1   Changes in Korean Population

Year	Male	Female	Total	Nationwide	Remarks
1913	39	5	44	3,635	
14	35	4	39	3,542	
1915	48	1	49	3,917	
16	68	–	68	5,624	
17	804	182	986	14,502	
18	913	109	1,022	22,411	
19	669	149	818	26,605	March 1 Independence Movement
1920	762	197	959	30,189	Rice Production Increase Plan
21	1,148	256	1,404	38,651	
22	1,399	282	1,681	59,722	
23	2,595	491	3,086	80,415	Great Kantō Earthquake
24	3,030	368	3,398	118,152	
1925	3,337	688	4,025	129,870	
26	2,707	748	3,455	143,798	
27	4,600	1,289	5,889	165,286	
28	4,590	1,281	5,871	238,102	
29	4,218	1,471	5,689	275,206	Great Depression
1930	5,541	2,264	7,805	298,091	
31	5,846	2,409	8,255	311,247	Manchurian Incident
32	7,816	2,973	10,789	390,543	
33	10,736	4,164	14,900	456,217	
34	12,286	5,641	17,927	537,695	
1935	10,671	6,745	17,416	625,678	
36	11,942	7,601	19,543	690,501	
37	11,772	7,753	19,525	735,689	China Incident Hiroshima Prefecture Concordia Society est.

Source: "Hiroshima Prefecture Statistical Report,"
Ministry of Home Affairs - Taken from *Current Social Movements*

Table 2　Changes in Korean Population During the War

Year	Male	Female	Total	Nationwide	Remarks
1938	15,573	9,305	24,878	799,878	National Mobilization Law
39	19,083	11,781	30,864	961,591	National Conscription Order Start of forced migration of Koreans to Japan
1940	24,143	14,078	38,221	1,190,444	Koreans forced to take Japanese names
41	31,324	17,422	48,746	1,469,230	
42	32,493	21,458	53,951	1,625,054	
43			81,863	1,911,307	

Source: *Current Social Movements*; however, figures for 1943 are from *Collected Materials Related to Koreans in Japan.*

end of 1944.

Unfortunately no accurate statistics exist on the number of Koreans in Hiroshima Prefecture brought over in forced-labor programs, but in the "Projected Number of Resident Koreans Wishing to Return to Korea" report (published in 1945), the number of so-called "general residents" at the end of 1944 was set at 75,919, while the number of so-called "group-immigration workers" (forced laborers) was recorded at 5,944.

Most of the Korean laborers forcibly brought to Japan were sent to work in coal mines in Hokkaidō or Kyūshū. Hiroshima Prefecture, which lacks substantial underground natural resources, had a relatively small number of these laborers, but it is generally believed that some were forced to work at power generating stations in the mountains and in munitions factories in the cities.

Korean A-bomb Survivors

The number of Koreans in Hiroshima on August 6, 1945, and the number of those actually exposed to the atomic bomb, remain rough estimates. It appears that 60,000 – 80,000 Koreans were living in Hiroshima Prefecture, and it is widely believed that one third to two fifths of these were exposed to the effects of the atomic bomb, 20 – 28% of whom died as a result. (The Committee for the Compilation of Materials on Damage Caused by the Atomic Bombs in Hiroshima and Nagasaki, *Hiroshima and Nagasaki: The Physical, Medical, and Social Effects of the Atomic Bombings*, Iwanami Shoten, Publishers, 1979.) According to the above estimates, 20,000 – 32,000 Koreans were exposed to the atomic bombing of whom 5,000 – 8,000 died.

These figures are the result of a comprehensive study published in 1972 by the Korean A-bomb Victims Relief Association (now known as the Korean A-bomb Victims Association), and information derived from death rates at given distances from the hypocenter, as well as from other written material related to Korean victims. These A-bomb victims were a mixture of general residents, students, workers recruited by the national mobilization programs, military personnel, military-related civilians, and laborers forcibly brought to Japan. After the war many Koreans returned to Hyopchon County in Kyongsangnamdo in Korea. A survey of those survivors has revealed that most Koreans were exposed to the atomic bomb and/or the ensuing radiation:

1) while in residential neighborhoods in western Hiroshima;
2) at other places within the city having entered from the outskirts;
3) at factories inside the city such as the Mitsubishi Shipyard (mobilized workers); or
4) in the city having entered after the bombing from draft labor factories just outside the city such as Japan Steel Works, Ltd.

[History After the Bombing]

After Japan's surrender on August 15, 1945, most Koreans were released and returned quickly to their homes. By March of 1946, thirty-five thousand Koreans had left Hiroshima

Prefecture for Korea. Consequently, the 1950 National Census indicates that the Korean population of Hiroshima City that year had dropped to only 4,729.

How many Korean survivors returned to Korea? According to the information published in 1972 by the Korean A-bomb Victims Relief Association (established in Seoul in 1967), 15,000 Korean survivors returned to the Republic of Korea, while 5,000 remained in Japan. Unfortunately, until recently we knew almost nothing about the survivors who returned to the Democratic People's Republic of Korea. But in 1995, the A-bomb survivors of that country formed the DPRK Anti-Nuclear Peace Consultative Council of Atomic Bomb Victims (Chairperson: Chu Song Un). Five representatives of that Association came to Hiroshima in October 1997. They reported the names of 730 A-bomb survivors in North Korea and revealed that, by the end of 1996, 180 of these were already deceased. (*Chūgoku Shimbun*, October 2, 1997).

In 1965, as part of the newly concluded Treaty on Basic Relations Between Japan and the Republic of Korea, the Republic of Korea waived all rights to war reparations from Japan. However, the Korean A-bomb Victims Association has continued its campaign for treatment and assistance to the Korean survivors who returned to their country. Since 1971, the National Council for Peace and against Nuclear Weapons has dispatched ten medical examination missions overseas. Both governments (Japan and the Republic of Korea) agreed in 1980 to allow short-term medical treatment trips to Japan. Under this agreement, 349 survivors came to either Hiroshima or Nagasaki for treatment by the year 1981. This figure, however, is but a small fraction of the 10,000 – 20,000 survivors supposed to be in the Republic of Korea. Furthermore, the program was terminated in 1986, thus making the situation even more difficult for Korean A-bomb survivors living in the Republic of Korea.

One positive incident, however, has been the Japanese

Supreme Court ruling in March 1978 in favor of Son Jin Du, a Korean A-bomb survivor (*hibakusha*) who entered Japan illegally, in order to obtain an A-bomb Survivor Handbook.

In April the same year, the Ministry of Health and Welfare responded by deciding that A-bomb survivors staying in Japan, regardless of any such reasons, should be eligible for the benefits under the Atomic Bomb Medical Law. This opened the way for A-bomb survivors residing outside Japan to obtain A-bomb Survivor Handbooks and receive medical treatment, when they come to Japan, regardless of the kind of visa or duration of stay.

When South Korean president Roh Tae-woo came to Japan in May 1990, a fund of ¥4 billion was established for A-bomb survivors in South Korea. This sum, to be disbursed in two portions of ¥1.7 billion and ¥2.3 billion, was to be used for 1) a health and welfare center, 2) a system of regular health examinations, and 3) continued payments from the national treasury for personal health expenses. (*Chūgoku Shimbun*, December 25, 1990). In October 1996, the Hapchon Welfare Center for A-bomb Survivors was built in Kyongsangnamdo, Hapcheongun. However, this accomplishment by no means solves the entire problem of A-bomb survivors in Korea.

A-bomb Survivors in the Democratic People's Republic of Korea

In 1995, A-bomb survivors in North Korea formed the DPRK Anti-Nuclear Peace Consultative Council of Atomic Bomb Victims. Five representatives of that organization visited Hiroshima in 1997 and appealed to the Japanese national government for an apology and compensation.

In 2001, a delegation from the Japanese government that visited North Korea to investigate the situation of the A-bomb survivors in that country reported that, "The North Korean A-bomb survivors organization conducted a survey in 2000 and confirmed that a total of 1,353 survivors were once living in North

Korea, and of those 928 are still alive." Subsequently, the DPRK Anti-Nuclear Peace Consultative Council of Atomic Bomb Victims announced that, "We have confirmed that 1,953 survivors returned to North Korea after the bombings of Hiroshima and Nagasaki." (*Asahi Shimbun*, July 4, 2002).

Chinese Survivors

Chinese A-bomb survivors also included students, soldiers, and laborers forcibly brought to Japan. The students were attending Hiroshima University of Literature and Science and the Hiroshima Higher School of Education. There were twelve of these students, one of whom was from Mongolia. Of these twelve, six were killed by the atomic bomb. (*Chūgoku Shimbun*, July 3, 1983)

The Japanese cabinet decided on November 27, 1942 to round up Chinese workers for forced labor in Japan. Chinese laborers were then forcibly taken to Japan and three hundred sixty Chinese workers were forcibly taken to work on the construction of an electric power plant in Yasuno Village in Yamagata County. One of these laborers suffered exposure to the atomic bomb after being arrested and jailed by the Hiroshima West Police Department for beating to death a fellow Chinese worker who was collaborating with the Japanese. The Hiroshima West Police Department was also holding five other Chinese for stealing and butchering a cow. They had been among the forced laborers taken to the power plant construction site in Yasuno Village. (Taken from: *Hiroshima Genbaku Sensaishi {Record of the Hiroshima A-bomb War Disaster*, Hiroshima City, 1971.}) In 1992, a group of private citizens known as the Chinese People Forced Labor Research Group conducted interviews in China and obtained testimony that "six people were exposed and died at the Western Police Station (Official Records state 5). Xu Li Chuang (69) and 12 others who had been in prison survived. At the end of 1945, they returned to China with 304 people who were still at the Yasunomura Power Plant where they had been forced to work." [*Yomiuri Shimbun*, June 13, 1992] One of those was Zhang Wen Bin (72), who was exposed to the A-bomb at Hiroshima Prison. He came to Hiroshima in May 1993 and was the first to obtain a survivor's handbook as a forced Chinese laborer.

On August 3, 1995, fifty years after the bombing, the first memorial service for Chinese laborers killed by the A-bomb was held in Peace Memorial Park. A number of bereaved family members participated.

The patient charts of the Hiroshima Army Hospital reveal that two Taiwanese soldiers or military-related civilians were hospitalized at that time. It is reasonable to assume that there were other Taiwanese in Hiroshima, possibly residents, students, soldiers, or military-related civilians, but the exact number is unknown. *Hiroshima and Nagasaki: The Physical, Medical, and Social Effects of the Atomic Bombings* puts the number of Chinese in Hiroshima at the time in a range of a few dozen to several hundred and estimates the number of A-bomb deaths at between 20 and 240.

Students from the South

In 1943, to train young people who were to help bring about the "Greater East Asia Co-Prosperity Sphere," Japan initiated a government program in which students from the Chinese mainland and Southeast Asia came to Japan to receive their education at government expense. In 1944, about 20 of these students from countries including Java, Sumatra, Borneo, Malaya, Burma, and the Philippines entered a special course at the Hiroshima Higher School of Education. They lived in the Kōnan Dormitory at 8 chōme Ōtemachi (now 4 chōme Ōtemachi). When the atomic bomb was dropped, nine students were in Hiroshima, eight of whom suffered some form of exposure to the bomb. Of these eight, two students from Malaya were killed.

American Prisoners

Toward the end of the war, American planes bombed the Japanese mainland intensively. The American prisoners in Hiroshima at the time of the atomic bombing had been flying over Japan in air raids and were shot down and captured. In July 1945, for example, a bomber crashed in the mountains near the village of Yahata, Saeki County, Hiroshima Prefecture, and two of the crew were sent to the Chugoku District Military Command Headquarters.

Initially, records kept by the Foreign Service Archives of the Japanese Ministry of Foreign Affairs listed the names and ages of 17 American prisoners who were believed to have experienced the atomic bombing at the Chugoku District Command Headquarters (according to the *Chūgoku Shimbun*, December 5, 1977). Other records in the same office indicate that 20 prisoners died in the atomic bombing. Later reports revealed, however, that nine of those had been killed in medical experiments at Kyūshū University or had been tortured and killed in Fukuoka. (*Chūgoku Shimbun*, July 24, 1978). Accordingly, the number of American prisoners who actually died in the atomic bombing would be eleven. Despite this, *Hiroshima Genbaku Sensaishi* (*Record of the Hiroshima A-bomb War Disaster*) placed the figure at 23, and *Hiroshima and Nagasaki: the Physical, Medical, and Social Effects of the Atomic Bombings* estimated that more than ten died by the end of August.

Japanese-Americans and Others

Hiroshima Prefecture is known locally as the "emigration prefecture." Over the years thousands of residents have emigrated, particularly to the United States mainland and Hawaii. Their descendants, born in America, became American citizens. Approximately 3,200 of these Japanese-Americans were in Hiroshima in 1945. Some returned to the U.S. immediately after the war, and their numbers plus the number of female atomic bomb survivors who married American men and moved to the U.S. totaled around 1,000.

Those Japanese-American survivors formed, in 1971, the Committee of Atomic Bomb Survivors in the United States of America. In 1977, the Japanese Ministry of Health and Welfare, in conjunction with Hiroshima Prefecture, Hiroshima City, and the Hiroshima Prefectural Medical Association, sent a team of doctors to examine those Japanese-American survivors. Similar teams have been sent to Canada (1983), Brazil (1985), and elsewhere in South America.

Two German priests from the Catholic Church in Noborimachi were injured in the atomic bombing but survived. There were also seven White Russians living in Hiroshima at the time who were exposed. One couple managed a clothing store in Kyōbashi-chō; a single man owned a bread shop in Kamiyanagimachi (now Hashimotochō); and a musician, his wife, and their children were also living in the city. Of these seven, one was killed.

Kaleria Drago (nee Palchikoff), a daughter of the musician, returned to Hiroshima in September 1986 after an absence of 41 years. In her testimony to the United States Strategic Bombing Survey immediately after the war, she stated, "We were exposed to the bombing in the Ushita area, and all four family members were safe;" "We were the only foreigners living in the suburbs. Everyone else was in the city. There were nine White Russians, a woman whom I believe was French, and twelve German missionaries." (*Asahi Shimbun*, September 30, 1986)

Assistance to A-bomb Survivors Residing outside Japan

According to the Ministry of Health, Labour, and Welfare, there are approximately 5,000 A-bomb survivors residing outside Japan, including about 2,200 in South Korea, about 900 in North Korea, and about 1,300 in North and South America.

In addition to medical treatment for those who came to Japan between 1980 and 1986, a medical assistance fund of 4 billion yen was provided for A-bomb survivors in South Korea (p. 153). Doctors from Hiroshima and elsewhere have been dispatched from Japan to offer medical examinations to North American survivors since 1977 and to South American survivors since 1985. In 2002, physicians from North Korea received training in the treatment of survivors in Japan.

Meanwhile, in 1994 two A-bomb-related laws were combined to form the Law concerning Support for Those Exposed to the Atomic Bomb (hereinafter, A-bomb Survivors Support Law), which went into effect in July 1995, the year of the 50th commemoration of the bombing. This law provided a new system for paying a special funeral allowance, and the income restrictions on health maintenance and other allowances were abolished. Moreover, it obligated the national government to perform some sort of memorial service for the victims of the atomic bombings. As a result of this provision, the Hiroshima National Peace Memorial Hall for the Atomic Bomb Victims was built in Hiroshima's Peace Memorial Park. It opened in August 2002. A similar facility opened in Nagasaki in July 2003.

In October 1998, Kaku Kihunm, a survivor living in South Korea, filed a suite in Osaka District Court against Japan and Osaka Prefecture for "cutting off my health maintenance allowance after my return to South Korea." In June 2001, the court ruled in Kaku's favor. As a result of this decision, the Ministry of Health, Labour, and Welfare began in 2002 to provide assistance to survivors living outside Japan, including the cost of traveling to and from Japan and also of staying in Japan for medical treatment, as well as medical examinations in their home countries.

The national government appealed the first decision to the Osaka High Court, but in December 2002, the High Court upheld the lower court's decision. The High Court ruling stated that the A-bomb Survivors Support Law was "a humanitarian law providing uniform relief for all special damage suffered by the *hibakusha*" and that "*hibakusha* are *hibakusha* wherever they may live."

The same month, the national government decided not to appeal the decision to the Supreme Court. Thus, the A-bomb Survivors Support Law officially came to apply to *hibakusha* living outside Japan. However, the A-bomb Survivors Handbook, possession of which is a condition for receiving all such benefits, can still only be obtained in Japan.

In April 2003, *hibakusha* groups from South Korea, the US, and Brazil gathered in Hiroshima and demanded that the procedures and medical benefits based on the A-bomb Survivors Support Law be realized in their countries of residence. (*Chūgoku Shimbun*, April 25, 2003)

Relief measures for the ageing *hibakusha* residing outside Japan must be improved still further.

Former president of the Korean A-bomb Victims Association appealing for Japan's generous relief at a gathering to support *hibakusha* residing outside Japan
(April 25, 2003, Hiroshima, Photo: Courtesy of Chūgoku Shimbun Newspaper Company)

Glossary

Glossary

Explanations of terms marked by an asterisk the first time they appear in the text (alphabetical order)

* Air-raid hood
A padded hood to be worn in air raids to protect the eardrum and head from blast and flying objects.

* Air-raid shelter
For protection during air raids, holes large enough to accommodate several people were dug into the earth.

* Air-raid warning
Warning by siren, radio, or megaphone indicating an imminent air raid.

* Akatsuki Corps
After the atomic bombing, this army shipping unit engaged in survivor relief activities.

* Army Clothing Depot
The Army Clothing Depot was located 2.67 kilometers from the hypocenter. During the war, it manufactured, mended, stored and distributed military uniforms, military shoes, military caps, and other apparel and accessories for soldiers. It was used as a relief station for some time after the bombing.

* Ashura (Asura)
In Buddhism an *asura* is a perpetually warring being. Someone who is always fighting is said to have fallen into the world of *asura*.

* Black rain
From 9:00 a.m. to 4:00 p.m. on August 6, muddy, sooty black

rain containing harmful radioactivity fell to the north and northeast of the hypocenter.

* Building demolition
To keep fires caused by an air raid from spreading, buildings were torn down to create open firebreaks. In Hiroshima, many students were working on building demolition when the atomic bomb was dropped. Thousands were killed.

* Civilian Guard
Civilian Guard units were organized in 1939 to protect people from fire, air-raids, etc. It was dissolved in 1947.

* Conpeitō
Small, round sugar candies molded in spiked spheres.

* Draft paper
Japan had adopted a conscription system in the Meiji era to enlist males in the army in case of war. The order to serve was called a draft paper.

* Drill ground
The grounds on which soldiers practiced military drills. Hiroshima had the Eastern Drill Ground (at Futabanosato near Hiroshima Station) and the Western Drill Ground (at Motomachi near Hiroshima Castle).

* Engineering Corps
This army unit built bridges in war zones, handled explosives, transmitted information and performed other engineering tasks.

* Firebomb
Firebombs kill by fire and burn down buildings. Because of the preponderance of wooden buildings in Japan, these were the

bombs the American military most commonly used in air attacks.

* Flea
This insect, 1 to 3 millimeters long, sucks blood through the skin of humans and other animals.

* *Fudō Myōō* (*Acala*)
This Buddhist figure symbolizing anger at the wicked is depicted in pictures and statues with a sword in the right hand and flames rising behind the head.

* GHQ
The General Headquarters of the Supreme Commander for the Allied Powers, located in Tokyo. The Supreme Commander was Douglas MacArthur, a general in the US army.

* Hijiyama Hill
This relatively low hill of 71 meters stands to the east of the Kyobashi River in Minami-ku near the center of Hiroshima City. The near side was approximately 2 kilometers from the hypocenter, and after the bombing many survivors took refuge there.

* *Hōanden*
Small, separate houses standing on school premises and used to safeguard photographs of the Showa Emperor and Empress and the Imperial Rescript on Education (a rescript containing the Meiji Emperor's prescriptions for morality and his basic policy on national education).

* Lice
A blood-sucking insect 1~4 millimeters long that usually lives in the hair of its host.

* Mobilized students
(See Student mobilization.)

* *Monpe*
Loose-fitting pants gathered at the ankle worn by women.
Monpe were worn alone or over kimono.

**The pants worn by the women working in the
rice paddies were called *monpe*.**
(Photo courtesy of Sadako Morisaki)

* *Muken-jigoku* (*Avici Hell*)
Jigoku is hell, where bad people go after death to suffer, and
muken-jigoku is the worst level of hell. The people in *muken-jigoku* cry and scream for relief from their extreme suffering.

* Mosquito netting
Finely meshed netting hung over bedding to protect sleeping
persons from mosquitos.

* National school
In 1941, elementary schools were officially named national schools. Compulsory education covered eight years: six primary grades and the first two secondary grades (ages 6 to 14) in national schools. The primary grades were renamed "elementary school" in 1947.

* National Volunteer Corps
A Cabinet decision in March 1945 laid the groundwork preparing Japan for a decisive battle on the mainland. This comprehensive national mobilization organization was charged with air defense, land defense, recovery from air-raid damage, increasing food production, and more. The groups targeted for membership were all graduates of the primary grades of national school, males 65 years or younger, and females 45 years or younger. Older persons could participate if they wished.

* Rations, Rationing
When goods became scarce during the war, the government prohibited the free buying and selling of commodities. Goods were distributed in fixed amounts to consumers through appointed organizations.

* School Evacuation Reinforcement Guidelines
(see School evacuations)

◎ School evacuations
When the US military invaded Saipan Island in June 1944, the danger of air attack on the Japanese mainland heightened. Then, bombers flew from American bases in China to attack Kitakyushu. In June 1944, fear that air attacks would intensify prompted the Cabinet (a minister-level council presided over by the Prime Minister) to establish the School Evacuation Promotion Guidelines to protect children in major cities from air attacks. The guidelines made stronger recommendations that

families participate in "connection evacuation" by sending children in the first and second grade of national school to live with relatives and friends in the countryside. They recommended that children in the third to sixth grades in national school with no relatives or friends in the countryside join in teacher-led school evacuations to temples and other facilities in rural communities.

American bombers did begin bombing the Japanese mainland from Saipan in November 1944, and the Cabinet decided the School Evacuation Reinforcement Guidelines in March 1945. These guidelines urged "connection evacuation" of even first and second graders in national school. Though "connection evacuation by all possible means" was recommended for third graders and above, students who could not find suitable people to stay with were forced to join the school evacuations. In Hiroshima, school evacuations began in April 1945.

◎ Student mobilization

Beginning in 1938, while Japan was at war with China, the national government ordered all students in middle school and above to work. After Japan began fighting with the US and its allies, most adult men were called up to fight, greatly shrinking the work force. (While Japan was at war with the US and its allies, it was also at war with China. Thus, the war is sometimes called the Greater East Asia War or the Asian Pacific War. This book uses the term "Pacific War.")

Because of the labor shortage, in August 1944 the Japanese government enacted the Student Mobilization Ordinance which formally mobilized even the lower grades of middle school and upper grades of national (elementary) school. Students were sent to work in factories, on farms, etc.

* Student mobilization Ordinance

(see Student mobilization)

* Women's Volunteer Labor Corps
This organization of female workers was created by the Japanese government during the Pacific War to compensate for the labor shortage. A government call in 1943 asked unmarried, unemployed women between the ages of 14 and 24 who were not in school to voluntarily join the Women's Volunteer Labor Corps. Later, the government more directly recommended that women join the Corps. The Women's Volunteer Labor Ordinance issued in August 1944 forcibly required all females between the ages of 12 and 39 to work for one year in a military factory or other workplace. (The period was later extended to two years.) In March 1945 this order was replaced by the National Labor Service Mobilization Law.

* Yellow Air-raid Warning
This warning informed people that enemy aircraft were approaching and an air attack could occur. (An air-raid warning meant that an attack was imminent.)

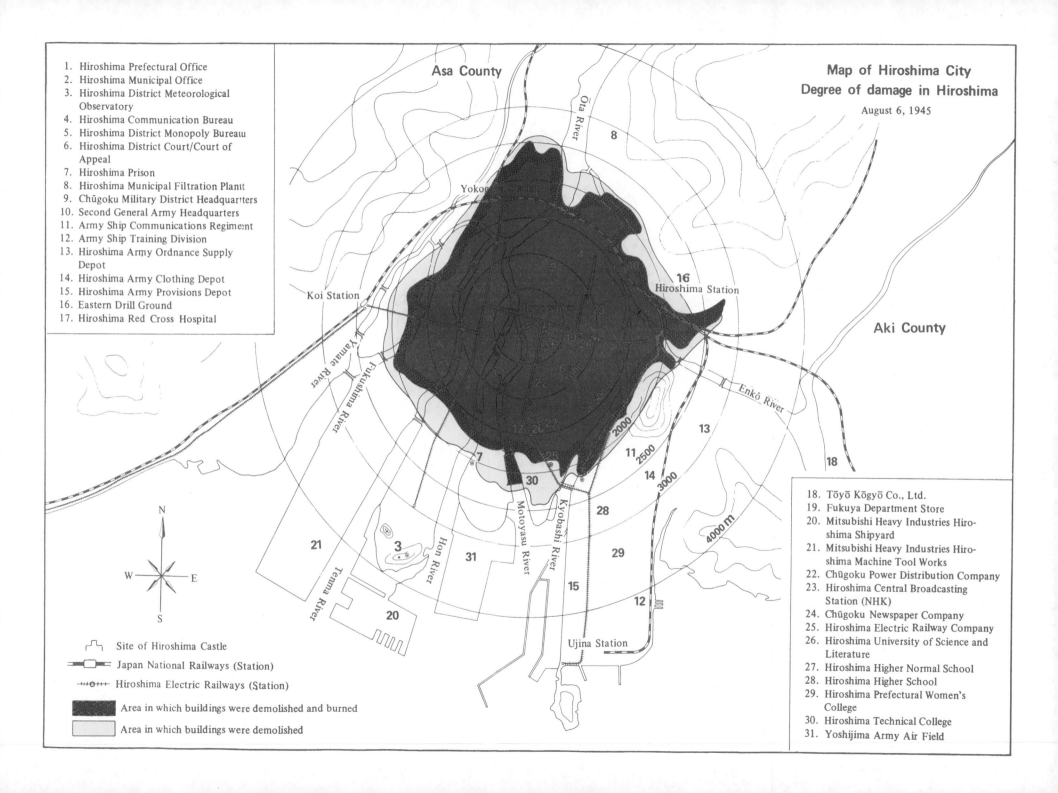

Map of Hiroshima City
Degree of damage in Hiroshima
August 6, 1945

Asa County

Aki County

1. Hiroshima Prefectural Office
2. Hiroshima Municipal Office
3. Hiroshima District Meteorological Observatory
4. Hiroshima Communication Bureau
5. Hiroshima District Monopoly Bureau
6. Hiroshima District Court/Court of Appeal
7. Hiroshima Prison
8. Hiroshima Municipal Filtration Plant
9. Chūgoku Military District Headquarters
10. Second General Army Headquarters
11. Army Ship Communications Regiment
12. Army Ship Training Division
13. Hiroshima Army Ordnance Supply Depot
14. Hiroshima Army Clothing Depot
15. Hiroshima Army Provisions Depot
16. Eastern Drill Ground
17. Hiroshima Red Cross Hospital

18. Tōyō Kōgyō Co., Ltd.
19. Fukuya Department Store
20. Mitsubishi Heavy Industries Hiroshima Shipyard
21. Mitsubishi Heavy Industries Hiroshima Machine Tool Works
22. Chūgoku Power Distribution Company
23. Hiroshima Central Broadcasting Station (NHK)
24. Chūgoku Newspaper Company
25. Hiroshima Electric Railway Company
26. Hiroshima University of Science and Literature
27. Hiroshima Higher Normal School
28. Hiroshima Higher School
29. Hiroshima Prefectural Women's College
30. Hiroshima Technical College
31. Yoshijima Army Air Field

Site of Hiroshima Castle

Japan National Railways (Station)

Hiroshima Electric Railways (Station)

Area in which buildings were demolished and burned

Area in which buildings were demolished

Ōta River
Yokogawa Station
Koi Station
Hiroshima Station
Yanate River
Fukushima River
Enkō River
Motoyasu River
Kyobashi River
Hon River
Tenma River
Ujina Station

N
W   E
S

Contributors (in alphabetical order)

Fumie Enseki	born in Hiroshima Prefecture in 1921 (deceased)
Setsuko Iwamoto	born in Osaka Prefecture in 1932
Kikue Komatsu	born in Osaka Prefecture in 1908
Seikō Komatsu	born in Hiroshima Prefecture in 1936
Miyoko Matsubara	born in Hiroshima Prefecture in 1932
Yoshito Matsushige	born in Hiroshima Prefecture in 1912
Hiroshi Sasamura	born in Hiroshima Prefecture in 1908
Akihiro Takahashi	born in Hiroshima Prefecture in 1931
Akiko Takakura	born in Hiroshima Prefecture in 1925
Chisako Takeoka	born in Hiroshima Prefecture in 1928
Taeko Teramae	born in Hiroshima Prefecture in 1930
Noriko Ueda	born in Hiroshima Prefecture in 1931
Toshiko Uehara	born in Yamaguchi Prefecture in 1947
Miyoko Watanabe	born in Hiroshima Prefecture in 1930
Rikio Yamane	born in Hiroshima Prefecture in 1908 (deceased)
Michiko Yamaoka	born in Hiroshima Prefecture in 1930

Other publications in English from the Hiroshima Peace Culture Foundation

A Photographic Record, Hiroshima ....380 yen

A Photographic Record, Hiroshima and Nagasaki ....500 yen

A-Bomb:A City Tells its Story ....400 yen

Hiroshima Peace Reader ....800 yen

An Introduction to the Atomic Bomb Tragedy by the Hiroshima Peace Memorial Museum:The Spirit of Hiroshima ....1,000 yen